on track ...

The Stranglers

every album, every song

Martin Hutchinson
Foreword by Baz Warne

SONICBOND
sonicbondpublishing.com

Sonicbond Publishing Limited
www.sonicbondpublishing.co.uk
Email: info@sonicbondpublishing.co.uk

First Published in the United Kingdom 2024
First Published in the United States 2024

British Library Cataloguing in Publication Data:
A Catalogue record for this book is available from the British Library

ISBN 978-1-78952-323-2

Typeset in ITC Garamond Std & ITC Avant Garde Gothic
Printed and bound in England

Graphic design and typesetting: Full Moon Media

Follow us on social media:
Twitter: https://twitter.com/SonicbondP
Instagram: www.instagram.com/sonicbondpublishing_/
Facebook: www.facebook.com/SonicbondPublishing/

Linktree QR code:

Acknowledgements

There are many people I'd like to thank for help, advice, information and encouragement. So, in no particular order, many thanks to the following:

Stephen Lambe at Sonicbond Publishing for having faith, Sil Willcox and Al Hale at Cruisin' Music, Gary Hibbert and Jerry Bloom at Wymer Publishing, Toyah Willcox, Alan G Parker, Steve Woof and Boo Hewerdine. I am particularly indebted to JJ Burnel, John Ellis, Paul Roberts and Jim Macaulay for their help and guidance. And most especially to Baz Warne, not just for the Foreword, but without whom this book would never have been finished.

Dedicated to my wife Michaela, daughter Emma and fur baby Sydney.

And in memory of my other fur baby, Darwin.

Thank you all!

Foreword by Baz Warne of The Stranglers

I've lost count of the times I've been asked about what makes The Stranglers so special.

The first 'classic' line up, the one that made all those fabulous (and a couple of maybe not quite so fabulous) albums, speaks for itself and was the beginning of the reason we're still here, nearly 50 years later.

They had everything, didn't they? A smouldering, karate chopping, hunky, punky French bass player, a sarcastic biochemist, an eccentric, pipe-smoking prog rock keyboard player with long hair and a droopy 'tache, and a forty-year-old drummer who probably should have known better.

All of them could give you a look that would curdle milk, and you'd probably think twice about approaching them on the street.

And the press that went with them at the time: misogyny, violence, belligerent sneering southerners who conquered wherever they went, taking your women in the process and giving you a smack if you so much as looked at them in the wrong way, dogged them for years. We all know the stories by now, and they were branded very much as outsiders. Too old for punk, but taking full advantage of the scene and using every bit of their pub rock training and nascent experience, they somehow forged themselves a following like no other – a following that's as strong, if not stronger than ever before, half a century later.

And yet through all that, through all the nonsense and mythology of those far-off days, the controversy and the hype, was the songs. The tunes; the riffs; the melodies; those fucking magic songs. They endure – will always endure-and when I'm asked, it's the obvious and only answer: the music.

Many of the old songs are bona fide classics. There are fan favourites, under-the-radar weird songs, pop singles, ten-minute prog workouts, disco, skewed reggae, acoustic ballads – the list goes on.

In my opinion, THAT'S what makes The Stranglers so special…

When you start a band, you want to sound like no other. You need to stamp your identity over everything you do so that when you're seen, or what was more likely in those days, heard, people instantly know it's you, and whether by design or accident, depending on who you speak to, The Stranglers stumbled onto a sound that was unmistakable and instantly identifiable as their own.

Over the years, that sound was honed, polished (sometimes too far – some of the eighties stuff was overblown and overproduced, some of even the hardiest of fans will agree), and then sometimes deconstructed again, but it was always them. Through the nineties, with the departure of Hugh Cornwell and the arrival of a different-sounding but equally good singer in Paul Roberts, the sound altered and shifted, but it was still undoubtedly them, and they wrote strong original-sounding pieces.

I joined in 2000, at a time when there was a struggle to keep direction while changing direction, but to still maintain the sound, to develop even more; very Stranglers – keep changing, but keep it yours, and keep it fresh.

I think we've managed to do that. From the moment I stepped through the door as an active member of the band, the songwriting process was, and is, taken every bit as seriously as it was decades ago, maybe even more so. Great care is always taken. It can sometimes take months to get things just right; sometimes, it can take twenty minutes. I can still remember my trepidation and nerves when I gave them my first song. I'd been in the band around three months and thought I'd at least better try to deliver something. I wrote a song called 'Dutch Moon' – it took about three-quarters of an hour. I thought that it couldn't possibly have been that easy, and worried incessantly over it, messing with it, tweaking and editing it, before I realised I'd maybe got it right first time, and just went back to the original demo. I gave each of them a copy at the airport the next time we were all together to fly out to a show. Jet called me a week later to say how much he loved it, soon followed by the others, and it was one of the first in the pot for the album that became Norfolk Coast. It also gave me great confidence to write more, and on my debut Stranglers album, I contributed four songs. Very satisfying.

Conversely, and right up to date, JJ and I had a song called 'Water' that took nearly a decade of messing with before we had it.

There's a song on *Dark Matters* called 'The Lines'. JJ and I wrote that in half an hour recorded it just once, live, the next day, with him playing acoustic guitar and me singing, just so we wouldn't forget it. It's the only recorded version in existence; we didn't do another and it made it onto the album just the way it was.

Sometimes, very rarely, that happens, too.

And that brings me to what I believe is the only rule of songwriting: never EVER throw anything away – ever. There are bits of songs, chord progressions, snippets of lyrics, riffs, melodies, etc., strewn all over the place and woven through so many of the songs I've been involved in and many that have gone before. Something you've written for one will often turn up in another, either whole or fragmented, or sometimes even just one word or passage. It would amaze you to know what's been written for a song, only to turn up somewhere else five years later. Any songwriter worth his salt will tell you the same – or should. Having said all that, there are also moments of unmitigated crap that are swiftly thrown out, never to emerge into the light of day again, leaving you wondering what on earth you ever saw in them in the first place.

You have to have your own strict barometer and vetting system – nobody is perfect.

I lose sleep agonizing over writing songs; JJ does too. We've been on the phone at ungodly hours trying to work stuff out, after having been with each other for a month and getting nowhere particularly fast, only to part, go home, fall asleep, then wake up shouting, 'I've got it'! Usually, the next day.

And so it continues. With two of the original band sadly no longer with us and a renewed lineup, we forge ahead. For however long is anyone's guess, but as long as we've got something to say, and a platform on which to say it – the fight goes on.

New blood brings different influences and diversities, and then, of course, there are our ages, which bring different perspectives and ideologies.

In The Stranglers, as I write now, all four members are in different decades of their lives: 40s, 50s, 60s and 70s. Is there another band alive and still operating that can say that?

Baz
December 2023

on track ...

The Stranglers

Contents

Introduction And Notes 11
Rattus Norvegicus (Stranglers IV) (1977) 16
No More Heroes (1977) 22
Black And White (1978) 28
The Raven (1979) 36
The Gospel According To The Meninblack (1981) 43
La Folie (1981) 50
Feline (1983) 57
Aural Sculpture (1984) 64
Dreamtime (1986) 72
10 (1990) 95
Stranglers In The Night (1992) 101
About Time (1995) 108
Written In Red (1997) 114
Coup De Grace (1998) 119
Laid Black (2001) 123
Norfolk Coast (2004) 124
Suite XVI (2006) 131
Giants (2012) 138
Dark Matters (2021) 142
Rarities 150
Compilations 153
Live Recordings 158
Solo Recordings 168
The Stranglers On DVD 169
Postscript 170
Bibliography And Selected Reading 171

Introduction And Notes

The Stranglers are a phenomenon. They were the top new-wave band (not punk!) and have been going for 50 years. In that time, the band have never split up, although there have been several line-up changes. As I said, they are not a 'punk' band. They were around a couple of years before the genre started, and they were a bit older than the bands that made up punk.

How does a band made up of an inventor and businessman, who, in his own words, left school 'barely literate', a biochemistry graduate, an Anglo-French martial arts expert who had read Economics and Social History at University, and a keyboard player who was a high-functioning autistic, become a band that has been reviled, respected, written off and lauded? Well, I hope to lift the lid a bit on the band and especially their music.

I will not be commenting on the band members' various idiosyncrasies and moods, nor will I go into too much detail on the touring – suffice to say that the band have toured their arses off for the whole of their career.

I have been aware of The Stranglers since their first hits. I was 17 years old when their first album and single were released and I have always liked their work – especially the singles as, in every song, there was something that set the band apart. It was quite a few years before I became a bona fide fan and started collecting their albums and seeing them live. I have also been lucky enough to interview JJ, Jet, Baz, Hugh, Paul and John, but not Dave, as he tended to only do interviews for keyboard magazines (although I have met him!). Every time I speak to one of the band members, I find them friendly and extremely helpful – a far cry from their early image of journalist-hating pranksters.

It is for that reason that I feel honoured to write a book about them. In this book, I have tried to examine – as far as I am able – the origins of the songs. For the most part, the writing credits always say 'written by The Stranglers', but then all The Beatles' hits say 'Written by Lennon and McCartney', which we know to be rubbish. It was Baz Warne who told me that, although one member may have had the original idea, all the band members contributed to the final track, and that is why all the credits (and royalties) go to them all – equally!

As with my first book, I shall be concentrating on the UK releases by the band and all opinions expressed in this book are entirely my own, although I must add that I do not personally side with the band in regard to any controversial topics that may arise in the lyrics. That said, let's get a 'grip' on the songs. I hope you enjoy it.

Formation

The story of The Stranglers doesn't start with their registration as a business on 11 September 1974; it began a few years before in Sweden when Hugh Cornwell formed a band called Johnny Sox. Hugh Alan Cornwell was born on 28 August 1949 in Tufnell Park, North London, and after gaining a bachelor's degree in biochemistry from the University of Bristol, he moved to Sweden to study for a PhD in Lund, a city near Malmo in southern Sweden. He was already proficient on the guitar, having played in a few bands, and whilst in Lund, he formed the semi-professional band Johnny Sox with guitarist Hans Axel Warmling (born 22 July 1943 in Gothenburg), bassist Jan Knutsson, singer Gyrth Godwin and drummer known just as 'Mike'. The latter two were a couple of American draft dodgers.

They were moderately successful on the local circuit but realised that they were never going to set the world alight from Sweden (this was just before ABBA proved that it was possible to set the world alight from Sweden) and, having renamed themselves Wanderlust, came over to England.

A number of personnel changes ensued, with Warmling returning to Sweden and Mike to the States. Mike's replacement was a former jazz drummer and local businessman, Jet Black. Jet was born Brian John Duffy on 26 August 1938 in Ilford, Essex. In 1997, this author enquired, during an interview, whether anybody still called him 'Brian'. His answer was a terse, 'My name is Jet Black'. 'Nuff said. He wasn't a good scholar, but was adept at chess and music, playing clarinet, piano and violin. After falling in love with rock 'n' roll, he moved to drums. He played all over the place but eventually settled in Guildford, where he set up his own business(es), amongst which were a beer and wine-making concern and an ice cream business (at one time, he owned a fleet of ice cream vans. He also ran an off-licence!). After a while, it became apparent to Jet that of the members of Wanderlust, only Hugh and himself were taking it seriously and had to either pull their socks (no pun intended) up or quit.

At the same time, singer Gyrth had been given a lift whilst hitch-hiking home, by a delivery van driver for a local firm. As a thank you, he invited the young man for a drink at the band's base – the off-licence. This young man was a karate-obsessed biker – and also a talented classical guitarist – called Jean-Jacques (JJ) Burnel. JJ was born in Notting Hill, London, on 21 February 1952 to French parents who ran a French restaurant. Due to being bullied at school, he anglicised his name to John but reverted to Jean-Jacques at the request of The Stranglers' manager Dai Davies. He read for a degree in Economics and Social History at Bradford University and was already into music and motorcycles (as well as women and drugs). At the time he joined the band, he was trying to save up the money for a trip to San Francisco and from there to Yokohama in Japan, where he wanted to win his black belt. He developed a lifetime love of Japan and its culture and is now a Black Belt 7th Dan in Shidokan Karate, the only 7th Dan in the UK. He also teaches karate and is head of Shidokan UK.

When Knutsson and Godwin left the band suddenly, Hugh went around to JJ's house and asked him to join the group and he had his audition in April 1974. As the band already had a guitarist in Hugh, JJ took on the bass guitar, buying a Fender Precision bass from Hugh.

Jet made them work for their board and the two frontmen were often seen behind the counter at the off-licence or around the town selling ice creams. He also sold all his ice cream vans to fund the fledgling band, except one, which served as the band's tour bus until 1977.

Hans Warmling eventually completed the first line-up as he came over to visit Hugh and was persuaded to join for his keyboard and guitar skills. He was also a talented writer, penning (with lyrics by Hugh) a song called 'Strange Little Girl', which was demoed and sent to EMI, along with 'Wasted' and 'My Young Dreams'. They were rejected, but the band had the last laugh as they re-recorded 'Strange Little Girl' as their last single for EMI.

The band left the off-licence and moved into a house in nearby Chiddingford and as Jet (still known as Brian Duffy) tried to get a recording deal, the rest of the band were pressed into bringing in some money. A local club took JJ on as a doorman and Hans as a dishwasher. Hugh signed on the dole.

The band performed gigs under a number of different names: Oil and The Slicks, The Chiddingford Chokers and The Guildford Stranglers, before finally settling on The Stranglers. Jet registered the name on 11 September 1974.

By this time, the band were playing a mixture of original songs and covers (one of which, notably, was Bacharach and David's 'Walk On By'), some rock 'n' roll standards and even the David Gate's classic 'If', recently a chart hit by actor Telly Savalas and given a live treatment by the one and only Jet Black. But it was the band's intention to cover 'Tie A Yellow Ribbon' by Dawn that led to the departure of Hans Warmling on the way to a gig. He returned to Sweden and did not meet up with his former bandmates until 1994. He sadly died in a boating accident a year later, on 12 October 1995.

The band soldiered on as a trio, but they knew something was missing. An advert was placed in the British music paper *Melody Maker* for a saxophonist and keyboard player. They hired a sax player, who only remained in the band for a few days and only played one gig. They started auditioning keyboard players. The third one they saw looked like a hippy and had been on holiday in Germany when his aunt had rung him to tell him of the *Melody Maker* advert. He was very proficient and played the songs like he had been rehearsing them for months. His name was Dave Greenfield. David Paul Greenfield came into the world on 29 March 1949 in Brighton and had a musical father. Although never pushed towards music by his parents, he became interested in classical guitar in his early teens. He then took a music theory course and taught himself to play the piano. Leaving school early, he spent a year in Germany playing gigs at American bases and clubs before returning home, earning money by tuning pianos and working in his father's printing business to finance trips to the continent to further his musical aspirations. He was a fan of The Beach Boys for their vocal harmonies and prog rockers Yes and classic rockers Deep Purple for their keyboard intricacies. Many people liken his playing style to that of Ray Manzarek of

The Doors, but he has always refuted that, saying that he was only aware of their hit singles.

A week after the audition, Dave made his debut as a Strangler and the rest of that year saw the band gigging and writing, supplementing their income by some diverse jobs. Dave and Jet teamed up to tune and repair pianos, JJ gave French lessons and Hugh taught biology at a local college.

In 1976, the band played no less than 191 gigs and they were slowly building up their fan base and reputation. They were often playing the pub rock circuit in and around London, where bands like Dr Feelgood sprang from. They played venues like The Hope and Anchor Pub and The Nashville, and quite often their support was a band called The Vibrators, whose guitarist, John Ellis, was later to become a Strangler.

The band's set was becoming dominated by their own songs, which would form the basis of their first two albums, but another aspect of the band was becoming apparent – the fact that many of their gigs drew some unsavoury characters and often there was violence at shows.

Here, I think I should mention two fans who were very supportive of the band. Garry Coward-Williams ('Chiswick Charlie') met the band in November 1975 when he was 15 and took pictures of the show. After the gig, Hugh approached him and asked to see the photos as the band needed some promotional shots. The band then took him under their wing and he even lived with them for a while. He also became a roadie for the band.

The other was 'Dagenham' Dave, who idolised the band after seeing them for the first time at The Golden Lion in Fulham. Dave was from Manchester, but Hugh named him after the Ford plant where he worked. He was adamant that the band would eventually make it, and The Stranglers themselves dubbed him their 'Number One Fan'.

Punk rock was coming in and although The Stranglers were never a punk band (I cannot stress this too highly), they got lumped in with the movement, frequently being banned from venues. In came another bunch of fans, which became known as 'The Finchley Boys' (guess where they were from). They installed themselves as the de facto fan club and private security force for the band. This put Dave's nose out of joint as he considered The Stranglers to be his band. He challenged The Finchley Boys to a fight one night and he lost, getting beaten up quite badly. Not long after, he committed suicide by throwing himself into the River Thames. The song 'Dagenham Dave' on the *No More Heroes* album is about him.

Punk was the 'in thing', and the media – and audiences also – thought of The Stranglers as a 'punk' band, even though they were older and more musically gifted than the others. The Sex Pistols and The Damned had been given record deals, and The Stranglers wanted one too. A number of labels turned them down, and they recorded a new demo tape with 'Grip', 'Bitching' and 'Go Buddy Go'. Manager Dai Davies contacted the A&R man at United Artists Records, Andrew Lauder, who had signed Dr Feelgood to the label. They arranged for him to see the band supporting Patti Smith at the Hammersmith Odeon, but the gig was a disaster with many technical issues (not the least being the old equipment that the band were using). They arranged a private audition at a rehearsal room on 4 December 1976. The Stranglers gave Lauder the works, and duly impressed, he signed the band to United Artists two days later, on 6 December 1976.

Rattus Norvegicus (Stranglers IV) (1977)

Personnel:
Hugh Cornwell: guitars, lead and backing vocals
Jean-Jacques Burnel: bass guitar, lead and backing vocals
Dave Greenfield: keyboards (Hammond L100 organ, Hohner Cembalet electric piano, Minimoog synthesiser), backing and lead vocals
Jet Black: drums, percussion
Additional personnel:
Eric Clarke: tenor saxophone (on 'Grip')
Recorded at T.W. Studios, Fulham, between January and February 1977
Producer: Martin Rushent
Engineer: Alan Winstanley
Original UK label and catalogue number: United Artists Records UAG 30045
Released: 15 April 1977 (UK)
Highest chart position: UK: 4 (Platinum), Australia: 82
Running time: 40:05
All tracks written by The Stranglers (Hugh Cornwell, Jean-Jacques Burnel, Dave Greenfield, Jet Black)

Upon signing the record deal with United Artists for £40,000 on 6 December 1976, the band descended on The T.W. Studios in Fulham and recorded all of the first album and quite a bit of their second. At the desk were United Artists' in-house producer Martin Rushent and the highly talented engineer Alan Winstanley, who would later take over production duties for the band.

Although gifted musicians, the four band members were very green when it came to working in a studio, especially as this one was a 24-track. They left it all to Martin and Alan (although it is said that Alan did most of the work). However, the first album was meant to be a live one, like UA's other pub rock band Dr Feelgood and their live album *Stupidity*. They even recorded their gig at The Nashville on 23 December 1976, but nobody was really happy with the result, so they went for a studio album instead. The band also needed some of their unreliable equipment updating and much of the advance for the album was spent on a new PA system and getting Dave's Hammond Organ serviced.

The name of the album also changed. The original title was to be *Dead On Arrival,* but when Paul Henry, United Artists' art director, found the image of a rat in the sunset, he thought that was the perfect image for the band. As the band were more 'intellectual' than most, they went for the Latin name for the Brown Rat as the new title (indicating that they were 'know-it-alls'), and in order to mislead the public, they added the 'IV' – just for fun.

With their live following gathering momentum, the initial release date of May was brought forward to April. *Rattus* was an instant success, reaching number four in its second week on the charts, eventually spending 33 weeks in the charts (17 of them in the top ten), and in the ensuing years, has gone platinum.

Hugh, JJ, Dave and Jet went straight out on tour and had no intention of slowing their pace down and would release another album in just five months.

There was a slight hiccup in July when JJ received his call-up papers for National Service in the French forces. He was commanded to report to Rouen in France to join the 39th Infantry Division. JJ escaped the draft by objecting, stating that it would conflict with his commitment to the band and proving his permanent residency in Britain.

'Sometimes'

This is an aggressive song and arguably one of the most 'punk' sounding on the album, although the organ gives it a nice melodic touch. Lyrically, it's about an incident in Hugh's life involving him slapping (once) a girlfriend after she cheated on him. After Hugh's initial idea, JJ came up with a strong and insistent bass line and then they took it to Dave and Jet, who added their parts. According to Hugh in *The Stranglers – Song By Song*, this was one of the earliest songs Dave worked on.

It became the first song on the album for two reasons. Firstly, it was the first song in the live set, and secondly, it brought the listener in, as the rest of the songs gave the listener something more intelligent to think about.

'Goodbye Toulouse'

This is one of those 'more intelligent' songs as it deals with the predictions of Nostradamus (Nostradamus [1503 – 1566] was a French astrologer whose book *Les Prophéties*, published in 1555, was a collection of 942 quatrains supposedly predicting future events). One of these predictions involved a catastrophe that would cause the French city of Toulouse to be destroyed. There is a nuclear power plant in the city and Hugh and JJ thought that a nuclear accident could cause the carnage. Hugh wrote the music and JJ the lyrics. However, Hugh sang the song as the bass line was too frenetic for JJ to play and sing at the same time. Essentially, they are saying goodbye to the city, and at the end of the song, there is an explosion denoting the meltdown.

Snarling vocals and the fast bass line give it a typical Stranglers feel and the organ is not as dominant as in 'Sometimes'.

'Goodbye Toulouse' was one of the four tracks recorded by the band for their first John Peel radio session, the other three being 'Hanging Around', 'I Feel Like A Wog' and 'Something Better Change'.

'London Lady'

This is a fast-paced (similar to 'Toulouse'), tongue-in-cheek song initially about a female journalist but was later aimed at ladies in a certain industry. This is very much a guitar-led song, with music by Hugh and lyrics and lead vocals by JJ. As well as a commentary on the antics of these 'ladies', there are references to drugs and punk's obsession with plastic clothing. The line, 'The lines around your eyes they show me you realise the party's over', denotes the short-lived career that the 'ladies' are in.

'London Lady' was the flip side to The Stranglers' first single 'Grip'.

'Princess Of The Streets'

The slowest song on the album is a 'swing' number in 6/8 time and is a song written and sung by JJ about a girlfriend. It's probably one of the most romantic songs JJ has ever penned, even though a hint of misogyny crops up in the line, 'What a piece of meat' (although JJ denies this).

Due to its 'jazz' style, the band were able to improvise a bit, especially Jet, who started out drumming in a jazz band. There are a couple of excellent guitar solos from Hugh and a keyboard run courtesy of Dave.

'Hanging Around'

These were the days when Hugh and JJ would write together. They usually sat in a room, just the two of them, and played around with ideas. On this one, the idea came from a bass line, with Hugh supplying the lyrics (except the fourth verse – those lyrics were by JJ). Most of the lyrics came from when The Stranglers had a residency at a club on the Mile End Road called The Nashville (where the aborted live album was recorded) and the people who frequented it (hanging around in the club). There's also a reference to Jesus hanging around on a cross, which is just Hugh being controversial. As with the majority of songs written by Hugh, he supplied the lead vocal. In fact, this was a trait with the band, with very few exceptions – whoever wrote the lyrics sang the song.

Dave has a bit of room to move on this track, and when the guitar solo starts (one of Hugh's favourites), he follows on. The song shows off just how musically savvy the band were, building from the initial organ intro to a crescendo.

This was slated to be the third single from the album, but with the second album, *No More Heroes* being released less than six months after *Rattus*, there was no time.

'Peaches'

JJ and Hugh wrote this song after spending an evening in a 'people of colour' club. They got immersed in the culture, and upon returning to their squat in Chiddingford (where they were living at the time), they wrote 'Peaches'. It was originally a reggae song, and certainly, the finished song still leans in that direction. In the book *The Stranglers – Song By Song,* Hugh describes it as a 'rap' song as there is no real singing on that or any of the other tracks on the vinyl records' second side. In fact, he was annoyed some years later when Blondie's 'Rapture' was lauded as the first 'rock rap' song.

The lyrics were by Hugh and they are full of sexual innuendos about ogling women. When selected as the second single, some lyrical changes had to be made for it to be played on the radio. Therefore, the word 'clitoris' was changed to 'bikini', 'oh shit' to 'oh no' and 'what a bummer' to 'what a summer'. Having said that, I am certain that despite the official lyrics stating 'peelin' skin', Hugh sings 'pubic skin'.

The flip side, 'Go Buddy Go', received the lion's share of the airplay due to it being more of an 'ordinary' (i.e. non-controversial) song and the band became the first 'punk' band to appear on BBC's *Top Of The Pops* (although they were not a punk band).

Speaking of their first appearance on the BBC's flagship music show, instead of trashing the dressing room, as the Beeb had probably expected them to, the band requested some cleaning materials and a vacuum cleaner. They tidied up after themselves before flying by helicopter to perform at a benefit gig at Colchester University.

The single, which was released on 6 May 1977 (United Artists UP36248), spent 14 weeks in the UK charts, reaching number eight and gaining a silver disc, and reached number 54 in Australia. Since then, it has been used in many TV shows: *Keith Floyd, Being Human, Gotham* and *Hollyoaks*, to name but four, as well as adverts and movies.

'(Get A) Grip (On Yourself')

One of the earliest tracks recorded for the album. According to Hugh, once the recording contract was signed, the band went into the studio and recorded this track and 'London Lady'.

This is another anthemic song about the time when the band were almost penniless and squatting in Chiddingford. For the uninitiated in British slang, a 'Morry thou' is a Morris 1000 car. It was quite a cheap car designed by Alec Issigonis ten years before the Mini. It was produced from 1948 to 1971, but by the mid-1970s, it was becoming a rare sight on the streets.

With lyrics by Hugh, this was the first single released by The Stranglers on United Artists (UP36211). The single was released on 28 January 1977 whilst the band were still in the studio working on the album. It spent four weeks on the chart and reached number 44. It should have gone higher, but due to a 'clerical error' at the UK Chart Compilers BMRB (British Market Research Bureau), the sales for the single in its fourth week in the charts were assigned to another record. Instead of heading into the top 20, it dropped to number 50 and lost its momentum. The band claimed that the act of sabotage was deliberate and the BMRB apologised.

The tenor saxophone on this track is played by Eric Clarke, a Welsh coal miner who was a friend of the band's manager, Dai Davies. Apparently, he finished his shift at the mine, travelled to the studio by train, recorded his part and then travelled back in time for his next shift.

The band had already recorded a demo of 'Grip' at a slower pace earlier in 1976. This older version appeared on a CD entitled *The Early Years – 74-75-76. Rare, Live & Unreleased* on Castle Classics (CLACD 401) in 1994.

A remixed version of the song, 'Grip '89', was issued with 'Waltzinblack' on the flip side (Liberty Records EM84). Remixed by Barry Cooder and Taff B. Dylan, the single reached number 33 in the charts during a three-week run in – yes, you've guessed – 1989.

'Ugly'

This was written and sung by JJ Burnel, with little input from the rest of the band. The lyrics are a bit dark, as they tend to suggest that 'ugly' people will only attract beautiful people if they're rich. He mentions a girl who was 'ugly', broad of hip and had acne. Apparently, he strangles her after she laced his coffee with acid. JJ had recently read the poem 'Ozymandias' by Shelley – hence the reference to that work (the band being 'know-it-all's again).

Musically, there's a great solo from Dave Greenfield, whilst the 'wooooo' noise is thanks to Hugh generating guitar feedback.

This song was very popular live; the band used to play it around three-quarters of the way through the set, giving them the chance to cut loose instrumentally.

'Down In The Sewer' (1. 'Falling' 2. 'Down In The Sewer' 3. 'Trying To Get Out Again' 4. 'Rats Rally')

This is a four-part magnum opus by Hugh and JJ, which runs just under eight minutes long. Hugh describes it as a suite with four movements and is mainly instrumental, which bears more than a cursory nod to prog rock. In the book *Song By Song*, he also states that the track is a 'classically structured piece', which further dismisses the notion that The Stranglers were a 'punk' band. It was a live favourite for many years.

It could almost be a follow-up to 'Grip', as it tells of the time the band were gigging in and around London, a bit further on from when they were in Chiddingford. The 'sewer' is an allegorical reference to the city, with the rats as survivors. Rats became almost synonymous with the band and the image of the rat on the back cover of the album is a symbol for the band.

A lot of the musical ideas are JJ's, with some sections (and the lyrics) by Hugh. Of the eight minutes, almost six and a half are instrumental, giving Hugh and Dave the chance to showcase their virtuosity on their respective instruments. Hugh, in particular, plays a guitar riff about half a minute in that would be more in keeping with Hank Marvin than a seventies rock band. The album ends with the squealing of rats and the drip-drip of water in the sewer.

Other Contemporary Tracks

'Peasant In The Big Shitty (Live)'

A live version of a track that would appear on the band's second album – and I'll go into it there.

'Choosey Susie'

This is a song by JJ and was the B-side of the free single given away with *Rattus*. The protagonist of the song – let's say JJ, for argument's sake – is trying to persuade Susie not to go home but to stay and indulge in some naughtiness (sex and drugs and rock 'n' roll). And yes, JJ did have a girlfriend at the time called 'Choosy Susie'.

This is a real rarity as it doesn't appear on any studio album, but there is a live version on the *Live At The Hope And Anchor* CD, which was recorded in 1977 but not released until 1992. It also crops up on the odd compilation.

'Go Buddy Go'

B-side to the 'Peaches' single. Okay, let's be honest, the single was 'officially' a double A-side written by JJ while he was still at school and is a straightforward rock 'n' roll song about a disco party, quite reminiscent in style of Chuck Berry, but inspired by The Beach Boys and Jimi Hendrix's 'Hey Joe'. When working on it, the band members thought it needed something extra, so Hugh provided a middle-eight and Dave chipped in with a superb keyboard run. The confusion about it being a B-side or double A-side came about when the radio stations decided that they couldn't play 'Peaches' (due to the suggestive lyrics) and flipped the disc to play 'Go Buddy Go'.

There is a story that, at an early gig at the Hope and Anchor, JJ's microphone failed during this song, so he walked off the stage to shout the words out to the audience individually.

This is another song that was demoed in 1976 (see 'Grip').

On the 50th anniversary tour, in March 2024, this song was the first of two encores played and was introduced as 'the first Stranglers song ever recorded'.

No More Heroes (1977)

Personnel:
Hugh Cornwell: guitars, lead and backing vocals
Jean-Jacques Burnel: bass guitar, lead and backing vocals
Dave Greenfield: keyboards (Hammond L100 organ, Hohner Cembalet electric piano, Minimoog synthesiser), backing and lead vocals
Jet Black: drums, percussion
Recorded at T.W. Studios, Fulham, between January and February 1977 and June and July 1977
Producer: Martin Rushent
Engineer: Alan Winstanley
Original UK label and catalogue number: United Artists Records UAG 30200
Released: 23 September 1977 (UK)
Highest chart position: UK: 2 (Gold), Australia: 79, Netherlands: 20
Running time: 38.01
All tracks written by The Stranglers (Hugh Cornwell, Jean-Jacques Burnel, Dave Greenfield, Jet Black)

The record company wanted to capitalise on the band's success, so they wanted the second album out quickly, probably before they self-destructed.

There were four tracks already recorded from the *Rattus* sessions: 'Peasant In The Big Shitty', 'School Mam', 'Something Better Change' and 'Bitching'. Of the rest, only two songs were new compositions: 'Burning Up Time' and 'English Towns'. The other five had been part of the band's set for some time.

The original idea for the sleeve was a photo taken of JJ lying on Trotsky's tomb (obviously not the real tomb, as Trotsky was laid to rest in Mexico). However, the idea was abandoned as the band didn't want any individual member standing out from the rest, and in the end, a photo of a wreath was used instead. Rather 'chintzy', it was still voted the sixth-best album cover of the year by *New Musical Express* readers.

There is a 'confidence' in the album that wasn't quite there on *Rattus*. This was probably because the band now had experience in the studio, plus Dave was more established in the band after previously being the 'new boy'.

The lyrics on this album are more 'nasty' than the previous effort. This was probably for two main reasons: firstly, the band wanted to wind up the press with their attitude, and secondly, as they were being linked with the punk movement, why not act like them?

The album also performed well chart-wise, reaching number two in the UK album charts, gaining a gold disc and spending 19 weeks on the listings.

'I Feel Like A Wog'

Despite the title, this is not a racist song. It is, in actual fact, anti-racist. Hugh, who wrote the song from a bass riff by JJ, uses the word 'wog' to denote alienation and being an 'outsider'. His delivery of the lyrics shows

Hugh's resentment at being treated as an outsider and identifying with the immigrants who had emigrated to Europe during the fifties and sixties.

The band were certainly not racist and often worked with black support bands like Steel Pulse. On one memorable occasion, Steel Pulse were receiving a lot of racial abuse at a gig in Birmingham, of all places. It got to a point where Jet Black took to the stage and berated the bigots.

The fast-paced song is quite 'jazzy' and all band members contributed to the final composition. It is the song on which Dave Greenfield uses a Moog synthesiser for the first time on a Stranglers' track.

'Bitching'

Everyone bitches about something at one time or another and this is The Stranglers venting their spleen. Lyrically, the song references the band's friendship with the Hell's Angels and some of the narrow-minded people the band encountered whilst trying to get gigs when punk bands were frowned upon (and again, I apologise for using the term 'punk' in relation to The Stranglers). Some of the venues the band played in early on are given a mention in the song, such as The Windsor Castle (no, not that one – this one is on Harrow Road) and The Hope and Anchor.

The intro of the song, which was written and sung by JJ, features every instrument that the band played at the time, and the medium pace allows for some great melodic moments during the solo. Of worthy mention is a memorable guitar solo.

This was also originally demoed in 1976 (see 'Grip').

'Dead Ringer'

The third song in and the third lead singer. Dave sings this, although it was a Hugh lyric, the reason being that Hugh's increased guitar work (he experiments with a few jazzy chords, which, together with Jet Black's ride cymbal accompaniment, give the song a swung feel) here rendered him unable to sing and play simultaneously. Apparently, Dave didn't need to be asked twice! In fact, Dave was the lead singer in one of his pre-Stranglers bands.

In the lyrics, Hugh comments on the fact that a lot of 'middle class' bands were trying to cash in on the 'punk' movement and people's need to follow trends so that they could fit in. The last line – 'Productivity. Credibility. Impossibility' – is Hugh questioning whether the band's high productivity is lessening their credibility.

'Dagenham Dave'

We're back to the 'pacier' songs for this one. With music from Hugh and lyrics by JJ, the song is about a friend of the band (the 'Dagenham Dave' of the title). The nickname was given to Dave by Hugh, despite the fact that Dave was a Mancunian. Dave was a massive fan of the band, and the song refers to a fight that he got into at the 100 Club with another group of Stranglers fans

– The Finchley Boys. Dave wasn't happy that they seemed to be taking over his 'crown' as the top fan of the band. Dave lost the fight, which sent him into a depression. He committed suicide soon after by throwing himself off Tower Bridge. As a final tribute to their friend, JJ said: 'I'm not gonna cry' because 'I bet he hit the water high'.

'Bring On The Nubiles'

Another song with questionable lyrics. At first glance, they are very misogynistic (not just 'at first glance', but every time you look at them, really). However, they were actually written as a 'wind-up' to see what the band could get away with. The song even hints at paedophilia ('I want to love you like your dad'). Apparently, Hugh had just read 'Lolita' by Victor Nabokov. Hugh and JJ would sometimes sing the chorus in a mock German accent ('Bring on ze nubiles') during gigs. 'Nubiles' was written during jamming sessions in the studio and when Hugh wrote the lyrics, he thought that he would never be able to put the word 'fuck' in a chorus to a song. This song is proof that he could – and did.

Songs like this and 'I Feel Like A Wog' are more 'in your face' and less melodious than most other Stranglers songs, and Hugh claims that he was goaded into writing it by the rest of the band.

The song, like quite a lot of tracks from the first four albums, is still very popular in the live set today.

'Something Better Change'

At one point during the summer of 1977, there were two Stranglers records in the top 30 charts in the UK, despite the lack of airplay on BBC's 'wonderful' Radio One. 'Peaches' was still in the charts, as was this double A-side (with 'Straighten Out'). This, the band's third single, was released on 22 July 1977 (UP36277). It peaked at number nine in the UK in an eight-week run and also reached number 29 in Holland.

This was arguably the band's only real stab at writing a 'punk' anthem, and an anthem it is. We have the organ intro, JJ's grunt and the instantly recognisable riff. Hugh's double-tracked guitar was at the suggestion of producer Martin Rushent, who wanted a wall of sound.

The lyrics are by JJ and it's a form of protest song, reflecting what was going on in the country at the time. The live audiences really get behind this song, except for one occasion in Japan. Hugh relates that during their first tour of Japan, this was the opening song in the set, and after playing it, there wasn't any reaction from the audience, so they played it again – and again. They played it eight times in a row before Hugh addressed the audience about it. Then, they started clapping and cheering.

'No More Heroes'

This was released as a single on 16 September 1977 on United Artists (UP36300). It spent nine weeks in the UK charts, reaching number eight and earning the band their second silver disc. It also reached number 25 in Holland. The B-side was a song called 'In The Shadows', a track that would appear on the next album.

One of the band's biggest and most popular hits, with the melody and lyrics by Hugh, this was created from one of JJ's amazing bass riffs and a memorable keyboard part from Dave.

The song bemoans the fact that all the 'heroes' of history and entertainment are no longer with us. In fact, the song was written just before the deaths of Elvis Presley and Groucho Marx (who both died in August 1977). The band wanted people to be their own heroes and not worship others. In fact, around this time, the band stopped signing autographs because of this. Of the people mentioned in the lyrics, Hugh was most fascinated by Leon Trotsky. While the band were in Los Angeles on a coast-to-coast tour, he realised that he wasn't far from Trotsky's house in Mexico, so he visited it.

The band performed 'No More Heroes' on Boxing Day 1977 on the Dutch TV show *Top Pop*. The show called for them to lip-sync to the song, so in true Stranglers style, they put two fingers up to them by having Dave on bass and vocals, JJ on drums, Jet on guitar and Hugh on keyboards. The clip is often repeated.

'Peasant In The Big Shitty'

Another lead vocal from Dave. That makes two on this album to make up for the fact that he didn't have a lead vocal on the first. The unusual timing of 9/4 meant that Hugh and JJ struggled to sing it. The pleasant guitar is counterbalanced with 'angry' bass and keyboards. It was written by JJ when the band were still living in Chiddingford and he was taking (according to Hugh) a lot of acid. The 'shitty', or 'city', is not necessarily London; it could be any large metropolis. As you can probably guess, it's about being poor (i.e. a peasant).

A live version of this track, recorded at The Nashville pub in West Kensington on 10 December 1976 using the Island Mobile unit, was issued as the A-side of a free 7" single that was given away with the first 10,000 copies of the original vinyl album. The catalogue number was FREE 3.

'Burning Up Time'

This was written by JJ, with the chords contributed by Hugh – who also supplies and sings a line or two at the end. The story, which is about JJ travelling on a train to see his girlfriend in Brighton, explores hedonism, declaring that you should use your time wisely as you haven't got much of it. The frantic tempo mirrors the rhythm of the train as it travels along the tracks.

'English Towns'

At the time of recording, the band regarded this track as a 'filler', written towards the end of the recording sessions when they were tired and the record company were pressing for one more song. As such, it was rarely played live. However, live versions do appear on *The Stranglers Live* (SPV Records), *Themeninblackinbrugge* (Coursegood Records) and as a bonus track on *Rattus Relived* (Coursegood Records) – although this is the same version as on *Brugge*.

This track is unusual in that it was written by JJ but sung by Hugh. JJ originally sang it, but Martin Rushent said that Hugh should sing it as it suited his voice better. The lyrics are about the groupies that hung around bands in the hope of having sex with the band members.

'School M'am'

Another song from Hugh that was developed from a bass line by JJ. The schoolmistress in question has CCTV in all the classrooms and spots a teacher having sex with a pupil. She watches until they climax, and then she climaxes also, but she is getting on and it kills her. During the performance on stage, Hugh would 'masturbate' his throat, then, at the climax, would unleash a stream of saliva to simulate orgasm. This was possibly (although not confirmed) the origin of fans spitting at punk gigs.

Other Contemporary Tracks

'Straighten Out'

This was the B-side of 'Something Better Change'. This is typical of Hugh from that time as he rails against society and the possible breakdown of order. It also criticises the British Government of the time, as headed by James Callaghan. This is another frantically paced song, but back then, a lot were. Actually, the whole song is a bit of a paradox, with dark lyrics and an upbeat melody.

When the Stranglers tribute band Four More Heroes disbanded, two of them formed another tribute band and named themselves Straighten Out.

'Five Minutes'

This was an A-side, released on 27 January 1978 on United Artists (UP36350), that reached number 11 in the UK.

JJ was inspired to write this, if that's the right word, by a flatmate of his being raped while he was away on holiday in Japan. While JJ vents his frustration at not being able to find the men responsible, the track also focuses on the big divide we sometimes have in cities. JJ's flat, which he also shared with Dr Feelgood's Wilko Johnson, was in a dangerous part of London but only five minutes away from the 'safe' haven of the affluent Bishop's Avenue with its' security cameras. On his return, JJ left the flat and it was taken over by Motorhead.

The song is a bit experimental sonically and a movement away from their more melodic numbers. The song ends with the sound of a ticking clock, and despite the title, falls short of five minutes by a minute and 43 seconds.

'Rok It To The Moon'

This was the B-side to 'Five Minutes'. It's a look into the future and Hugh (whose song it was) doesn't want to be here – he wants to look upon it from a distance. A bit weird this one, with keyboard effects and intermittent trills on the guitar. Hugh wrote it after seeing the band Devo, whose style was then rather robotic. The Stranglers had discovered cocaine by now, which led to some lengthy theorising about all sorts of subjects, this being one of them.

Black And White (1978)

Personnel:
Hugh Cornwell: guitars, lead and backing vocals
Jean-Jacques Burnel: bass guitar, lead and backing vocals
Dave Greenfield: keyboards (Hammond L100 organ, Hohner Cembalet electric piano, Minimoog synthesiser), backing and lead vocals
Jet Black: drums, percussion
Additional personnel:
Lora Logic: saxophone on 'Hey!'
George Melly: vocals on 'Old Codger'
Lew Lewis: harmonica on 'Old Codger'
Recorded at T.W. Studios, Fulham, in July 1977 and between February and March 1978
Producer: Martin Rushent
Engineer: Alan Winstanley
Original UK label and catalogue number: United Artists Records UAK 30222
Released: 12 May 1978 (UK)
Highest chart position: UK: 2 (Gold), Australia: 81, Sweden: 35
Running time: 39.50
All tracks written by The Stranglers (Hugh Cornwell, Jean-Jacques Burnel, Dave Greenfield, Jet Black)

Black And White was the first album to be comprised of 'new' compositions from the band. The majority of the first two albums were songs perfected over three years of gigging. For this one, they had to start from scratch and they started being experimental with unusual tempos ('Curfew') and inspiration from obscure sources.

The band started working on the songs in December 1977 at the Bear Shank Lodge in Oundle, Northamptonshire. To escape the cold, Hugh went on holiday to Morocco, where he wrote many of the album's lyrics. Just before this, two of the band members, JJ and Jet, had their first taste of prison cells when they were charged with obstruction and spent a night as guests of the local police (they were trying to help a couple of the members from the Dutch Hell's Angels who had been arrested at a gig at the Top Rank Brighton).

The original plan was to have a white side (JJ's music and Hugh's lyrics) and a black side (Hugh's music and JJ's lyrics). Tracks one to six were classed as the 'white' side of the album and the rest as the 'black' side'.

The first 75,000 copies of the album came with a free three-track single on white vinyl of 'Walk On By', 'Mean To Me' and 'Tits'. The US version was released by A&M Records and was on black and white marbled vinyl but offered no free single. The CD versions (except a reissue in 2018) had 'Hey!' coming after 'Outside Tokyo' and 'In The Shadows' coming after 'Threatened'.

The press launch for the album was in Iceland and it was here that the band started to get their own back on some of the journalists who had – shall we say – upset them with their comments. Promotional photographs were taken with the grandeur of the Icelandic volcanoes in the background and the band being hung very far over.

For one journalist, however, this jaunt was to result in the end of his career. The gentleman in question (who shall remain nameless, mainly because nobody can remember his name) challenged JJ to a drinking contest. The journalist lost; in fact, he lost so badly that he ended up comatose in a wheelchair and was refused entry onto the plane home. He lost his job as a result. Despite this, the album was well-received by critics.

After the photo shoot, where the band wore predominantly black, they started wearing all black when most new-wave acts were wearing bright colours (The Stranglers had to be different, you see). This also created the image that the band were 'threatening'. At the time, JJ said, 'They do say that black clothes create negativity, so I always make sure I wear some non-black just to fight it off'. The band were transitioning from a new wave to a more 'adult' approach, and their management were against it. This eventually led to the band parting company with them.

This album was also different production-wise. On the first two albums, producer Martin Rushent's brief was 'don't produce it', as the record company wanted to capture the energy of a live Stranglers performance on vinyl. On this album, he was allowed to have more input, which led to arguments with the band, and eventually, he walked out.

The album cover is just a black and white photograph of the band, taken by Ruan O'Lochlainn, but with no title or band name (which was brave), and was creatively called *Black And White*.

'Tank'

This was one of the tracks on the B-side of the 'Walk On By' single, along with 'Old Codger'. It was originally meant to be a double A-side, but all the attention went to 'Walk On By'.

A Hugh lyric from a JJ bass line (sound familiar? This was also the case for 'Nice 'N' Sleazy', 'Outside Tokyo' and 'Sweden'), this is one of the lyrics that Hugh wrote at the lodge rather than in Morocco. He said that he likened being on the road to being in the military and being in the military means you can drive a tank.

This song is very fast-paced, with the fastest keyboard riffs in rock. Dave's arpeggios aren't done on a synthesiser but on his trusty Hammond organ, and it could be said that 'Tank' is halfway between the sometimes-frenetic style of the first two albums and the more melodic sound of Black And White.

'Nice 'N' Sleazy'

This is the A-side from the first single taken off the album, released on United Artists (UP36379) on 26 April 1978. It climbed to number 18 in the UK and spent eight weeks on the charts. In fact, we were entering a period of low returns on singles. Whilst every single released from 1977 to 1992, bar one, entered the charts (making The Stranglers one of the most successful chart bands ever), there would only be four more to hit the UK top ten.

Another attempt by the band at 'white reggae', it succeeds where 'Peaches' failed by having a more authentic reggae sound (JJ said that 'we fucked up on 'Peaches'.) I'd say that it was almost a 'son of *Peaches*'. A highlight here is Dave's Moog sweeping from speaker to speaker.

The first verse is about the band's first visit to America, whilst the second is about encountering Hell's Angels in Amsterdam. The title is a satire on Frank Sinatra's *Nice 'N' Easy*. It was reported at the time that Sinatra's lawyers threatened to sue United Artists over it, but the record company ignored the threat and nothing else was heard.

At a gig in Battersea Park on 16 September 1978, the band booked strippers to 'perform' during the song. However, some of the males in the audience (allegedly The Finchley Boys) got carried away and stripped completely naked, leading to a call to the police.

The title also lives on in the name of a Morecambe Punk festival and a bar in Glasgow.

'Outside Tokyo'

Hugh has always been fascinated by time and this song is about that. We are in a watch factory that makes millions of watches. But if no more watches were made – according to the theory in the song – there would be no time as we wouldn't have the means to measure it.

According to *The Record Mirror*, the song's riff is 'funereal'; however, to my ears, it's more like a waltz (and, of course, a song in waltz time would be very successful for The Stranglers in a few years).

'Sweden (All Quiet On The Eastern Front)'

This was inspired in part by Hugh's placement at Lund University in Sweden in the early seventies and a gig on a Swedish tour that was violently interrupted by some Swedish rockers known as The Raggare. The line about 'Big Brother' refers to Hugh's perception of the Swedish government and their control over its citizens. For instance, while he was living there, the government changed the side of the road you were supposed to drive on. They stopped traffic completely at 4 pm one day and changed all the road signs overnight. The population's obedience meant that there were no accidents following the change.

The song has some dramatic pauses and changes in tempo, which sometimes make you feel as if there are two separate songs going on. The tempo seems to stop and start, the slower parts denoting the tedium that Hugh felt in Sweden. The band also recorded the song in Swedish and released it as a single there.

'Hey! (Rise Of The Robots)'

The lyrics were written by Hugh for a piece of music created during a jam session in the studio. Hugh had just read Isaac Asimov's book *I, Robot*, which chronicles the rise of robot technology. He decided to mix up the lyrics in order to portray the fact that without humans programming them, robots cannot communicate correctly. He also references the Tin Man from *The Wizard Of Oz*.

There's a lot going on musically (metallic sounds and a feeling of disorder are underlined by the seemingly random use of saxophone) and it's very fast – almost frantic. This made the song difficult to mix because of the different sections of the song. In 2001, Hugh called it a 'complete mess'. It was JJ who thought that it would be a good idea to include a mad saxophone solo on the track, so they brought in Lora Logic, the saxophonist from punk band X-Ray Spex.

'Toiler On The Sea'

More proof, if that was needed, that The Stranglers were more than your average band with average intellects. Hugh was, and is, very well-read. This song refers to Victor Hugo's novel *Toilers Of The Sea*, published in 1866, and is – in effect – a love story.

The lyrics refer to the holiday in Morocco that Hugh and his girlfriend took during the Christmas break while working on the album. He was dogged by bad luck. The 'aliens' that Hugh refers to appear to be the airport authorities, whom Hugh had an argument with. The lyric, 'the young ones used their hands', was a reference to the fact that a child stole his girlfriend's money. Then, for good measure, Hugh and the girl split up soon after returning.

The guitar solo came from a melody by JJ and was Hugh's attempt at recreating the sound of The Shadows, a band that Hugh admired. It's another fast-paced number, which was really the norm for The Stranglers in 1977. Dave supplies a couple of excellent keyboard runs.

A piece of trivia: the band A Flock Of Seagulls took their name from this song.

'Curfew'

This is another very clever piece of music with some changes in time signatures – the verses are in 7/4 time and the choruses in 4/4. Dave enhances Hugh's brilliant music with a sublime keyboard riff. The intervals in the music have always been associated with satanism and darkness (they also crop up in the next track 'Threatened'), due to the dissonance going against the more harmonious sound. It was given the name 'diabolus in musica' (The Devil in music).

The song is a bleak account of a political breakdown, and in the last verse, JJ references the post-war division of Germany. Lyrically, this is a true Cornwell/Burnel collaboration, as Hugh wrote the chorus and JJ the verses. In the song, JJ puts himself in the boots of an Army officer, telling the populace to 'Stay in your homes/Be off the streets by nightfall'. And with the words, 'The Government has fled to Scotland today', he denotes that, in this scenario, Scotland is an independent nation.

'Threatened'

With lyrics from JJ (except the last verse, which was Hugh), this song is about paranoia. Both JJ and Hugh were unsure about their future at the time. This was arguably a 'make or break' album, being almost totally made up of brand-new material, and this feeling comes across in the words.

At the start of the track, the music slowly builds up with Jet's syncopated drumming (actually, the syncopation was created in the studio by Martin Rushent and engineer Alan Winstanley, who set up a slight delay on the drum). The song has a steady, mid-tempo rhythm throughout. Dave Greenfield prefers to favour the Mini Moog synthesiser on this track more than the Hammond organ or Cembalet, and Jet indicates the approaching threat by use of the hi-hat to create the 'ticking' sound.

'Do You Wanna'

This is another song that originated from a jam session. Hugh wrote the lyrics, but because of the complicated guitar part, it's sung by Dave. Hugh has said that, in his opinion, the bass is so loud in the mix that you can hardly hear the guitar part. This author's personal opinion is that, although the bass does indeed overshadow the guitar, it's an important part of the music – in fact, a trademark of The Stranglers.

The song is about possibilities and the things you could do if the chance came. There's also a dig at the establishment and the fact that there were no prisoner's amnesties granted as part of the jubilee celebrations (1977 was Queen Elizabeth II's Silver Jubilee) as there had sometimes been in the past.

Then, at the end, the track seamlessly crossfades into...

'Death And Night And Blood (Yukio)'

This was inspired by Yukio Mishima's novel *Confessions Of A Mask*, which was published in 1949. JJ wrote the lyrics with the music coming from Hugh.

Mishima was one of JJ's heroes, and he (Mishima, not JJ) and his followers obeyed the ways of the Spartans, an ancient warrior race (hence the mention in the lyrics). It's a rather anthemic song, with the band chanting 'death and night and blood'. It's definitely one of the band's more sinister-sounding tracks.

'In The Shadows'

Yet another one showing off The Stranglers' more 'sinister' side. It's also quite experimental, being synth-led rather than guitar-led. It, therefore, gives a small hint at the things to come for the band.

The song was recorded in July 1977, over six months before the rest of the album, and was the B-side to the single 'No More Heroes', which had been released the previous September. It was recorded in just one day, with the band first recording the bass and drums jamming together for five minutes or so (the final track time was 4.15). Hugh then added his guitar and then Dave his 'psychedelic' keyboards. After that, Hugh slotted in his lyrics. Mr Cornwell later said that this track gave him the chance to be a bit like Syd Barrett from Pink Floyd with the darker overtones.

As this track had been laid down straight onto tape in the studio, the band had to listen to it again and again so they could learn their respective parts in order to be able to perform it live. Producer Martin Rushent had no input on the song as he wasn't in the studio when they put it together and reportedly wasn't keen on what the band had created.

Lyrically, it does what it says on the tin (in the title). It's about what you imagine seeing in the shadows when walking the streets at night.

'Enough Time'

'Enough Time' is another song where the bass almost drowns out the guitar. Like 'English Towns' on *No More Heroes*, it was written right at the end of the recording sessions. I'm wondering if the same initialling on the two songs is more than a coincidence.

The track was developed by a JJ bass riff, and with it being written at the end of the sessions when the band were tired, writing the lyrics was apparently hard work. As a result, they are quite dark and deal with the fallout from a nuclear explosion. It's also a bit graphic, with the lyric 'when your face falls apart' being particularly harrowing. Just after the two-and-a-half-minute mark, we get a distress call in Morse code, which adds to the atmosphere.

The lead vocal (from Hugh) and music decrease in tempo at the end of the song, denoting the fact that time is running out, whilst JJ's voice gets higher by being put through a harmoniser.

Other Contemporary Tracks

'Mean To Me'

This was included on the free EP that came with the first 75,000 copies of the vinyl release but was left off the actual vinyl album! Yet, it was included on the cassette version.

A Hugh song written in about 15 minutes (he says), it's a basic 12-bar song and was played at a lot of the early pub gigs and is a typical early Stranglers thrash.

Before The Stranglers recorded it for the album, the song was recorded and released by Celia & The Mutations. Celia was singer Celia Collin, who had been 'discovered' by The Stranglers' then-manager Dai Davies. The A-side was a cover of Tommy James & The Shondells 'Mony Mony', but

'Mean To Me' was a Stranglers song, and on this single, The Mutations were, in fact, The Stranglers. Despite a vigorous advertising campaign, where 'The Mutations' were illustrated in silhouette (actually a silhouette of The Stranglers from the back cover of *Black And White*), the single failed to trouble the chart compilers.

'Walk On By' (Burt Bacharach, Hal David)
This was a live favourite that had been in the band's set for a few years (it was even being performed by the band when Hans Warmling was with them). The song had evolved, growing from the original band thrash to a more refined song. The version on the album is over six minutes long and includes extended guitar and keyboard solos.

In May, the band gave away 75,000 copies of the song (along with 'Mean To Me' and 'Tits') on a free EP with the *Black And White* album. The catalogue number was FREE9. However, after two months, the demand for the song was so great that United Artists decided to release it as a single (UP36429) with 'Old Codger' and 'Tank'. However, it appeared that the free issue might have affected the sales as it only reached number 21 on the UK Singles Chart and number 11 in Ireland.

Written by Burt Bacharach and Hal David, the song had previously been an international hit for Dionne Warwick.

'Shut Up' (Demo)
This was released as the B-side to the single 'Nice 'N' Sleazy'. Coming in at just one minute and seven seconds, it is the shortest song that The Stranglers recorded. Another Stranglers assault on the ears, it was always regarded by the band as a 'filler'. Written by JJ, it is about being fed up with someone talking to you and wanting them to 'shut up'.

'Sverige (Jag Ar Insnoad Pa Ostfronten)' (Stereo Alternate Take)
This is the song 'Sweden' sung in Swedish. It was released as a single in Sweden by United Artists (UP36459), with 'In The Shadows' on the flip side. It didn't chart.

'Old Codger'
This was also one of the tracks on the B-side to 'Walk On By' when issued properly as a single. It features jazz singer and raconteur George Melly as lead vocalist and Lew Lewis, who had played with Eddie & The Hot Rods and Dr Feelgood, on harmonica. The band had met George Melly when taking part in a BBC Arts programme and had got on very well. Hugh wrote the song about George (who was bisexual) being a dirty old man and trying to pick up choirboys. Melly liked the lyrics, agreed to do the vocals and even supplied an ad-lib at the end of the song.

The song was occasionally performed live, with Jet Black as vocalist.

'Tits'

This track was included on the free EP given away with the album. Originally entitled '36-24-36', it was recorded live at the Hope and Anchor on 22 November 1977. 'Tits' was easier to write on the setlist, hence the name change. In the end, it was a good job they renamed it, as American singer Bobby Bland also released a song with the same title, yet strangely, he never got blasted with accusations of misogyny as The Stranglers did.

Played in a sort of 'swing' style, this song was only ever performed live and never recorded in a studio. Hugh uses the song to introduce the band and they all have a little solo.

The Raven (1979)

Personnel:
Hugh Cornwell: guitar, vocals, second bass on 'Dead Loss Angeles'
Jean-Jacques Burnel: bass guitar, vocals
Dave Greenfield: keyboards, vocals
Jet Black: drums
Recorded at Pathe Marconi Studios, Paris, in June 1979
Producer: The Stranglers and Alan Winstanley
Engineer: Alan Winstanley
Original UK label and catalogue number: United Artists Records UAG 30262
Released: 15 September 1979 (UK)
Highest chart position: UK: 4 (Gold), Australia: 71
Running time: 41.11
All tracks written by The Stranglers (Hugh Cornwell, Jean-Jacques Burnel, Dave Greenfield, Jet Black)

After the first three albums were released in the space of 13 months, we had to wait 16 months before the next album. In the interim, the live album *Live (X-Cert)* had been released – but we'll come to that later. The band hadn't had such a long break in between recording sessions before, and as a result, they were more relaxed. However, in that gap, the band toured America, Australia, Japan and Europe. JJ had recorded his first solo album *Euroman Cometh*, and on 16 September 1978, the band performed an open-air gig in Battersea Park where strippers came on during 'Nice 'N' Sleazy'. The police were called, but no action was taken in the end. The ban on 'punk' artists was at its height and The Stranglers were affected by this – they overcame it by appearing at gigs using other names.

The album was heralded, a month before release, by the single 'Duchess'. A month after release came the single 'Nuclear Device'. Then, in November, came the EP *Don't Bring Harry*. The album was written in Perugia, Italy, at the home of the father of JJ's then-girlfriend. Both JJ and Dave drove there, but Jet and Hugh decided to take the train, which, according to Hugh, was 'horrendous'.

The album deals with a number of topics, from their travels around the world to aliens and cannibalism (and the latter two in the same song). JJ named the album *The Raven* as, firstly, they had already written the song 'The Raven', and secondly, JJ was interested in Norse mythology, in which the raven is a very potent symbol; they were the 'eyes' of Odin and the Vikings took ravens on their voyages to look for new territories. Also, by now, the band had become 'the men in black', or rather 'themeninblack', and the raven is a black bird.

This is an album of which all four of the band members are proud and were dismayed when, due to a clerical error, the sales of the album were credited to *Regatta De Blanc* by The Police. This album got to the top of the charts. This is strange as The Police's album had yet to be released! ***The Raven*** still managed to get to number four and earned the band another gold disc. But it was the first album by the band to spend less than ten weeks in the charts, dropping out after eight.

The first 20,000 copies of the album had a 3D image of a raven on the sleeve, which always appeared to be looking at you. On the reverse was a band photograph taken in a Viking longship (actually, on concrete blocks near Ramsgate.). The 3D image was created in Japan and featured three photos of the same image printed on a serrated sheet to give a 3D effect. After the first 20,000 were sold, the image was the same, but a 2D painting.

The band launched the album at a gig supporting The Who at Wembley Stadium. The Stranglers' fireworks were so powerful that The Who were banned from using their own pyrotechnics during their set. This must have irked The Who's guitarist Pete Townshend, as he had been less than complimentary to The Stranglers in the music press the previous year.

Sadly, the T.W. Studios, where they had recorded the first three studio albums, had closed, so ***The Raven*** was recorded at the Pathe Marconi Studios in Paris. Following the departure of producer Martin Rushent, the band co-produced the album with Alan Winstanley, who had engineered the first three albums.

Amazingly, the band's management team of Dai Davies and Derek Savage suggested to the band that it might be best if the band split up as they thought they had run their course, but the four band members foresaw further success in the pipeline. This was the beginning of the end for the managers, as the band thought that they didn't believe in them anymore.

In the same month that ***The Raven*** was released, Hugh, in collaboration with Robert Williams – the drummer for Captain Beefheart – released the album *Nosferatu*.

'Longships'

We have an instrumental to open the album, and it's very nearly the shortest track ever by the band ('Shut Up' is shorter by just three seconds).

It was written by Hugh, but he couldn't think up any lyrics to go with it, so the band left it as an instrumental – an eccentric waltz in 4/4 time. Personally, I think it could have at least been used as an intro to a song.

'The Raven'

The title track to the album has lyrics, vocals and a bass riff from JJ, whilst Dave and Hugh worked out their own parts. Jet apparently had free rein to work out his percussion parts to every song. The song has a longish intro (like 'Ice' and 'Shah Shah A Go Go') with all the band coming in together, rather than previous ling intros where they tend to come in one by one. In particular, Dave's keyboard riff is very memorable.

The song could well be a metaphor for the band going out on tour. At this point in their career, The Stranglers were often the first band to play at a newly established venue, so they were trailblazing for the rest, much like the ravens that were carried on board the Viking longships and sent out to look for land.

'Dead Loss Angeles'

This features another lyric from Hugh outlining the band's experience of America, the title being a play on the words 'dead loss' and 'Los Angeles'. There are references to Lake Michigan and the La Brea Tar Pits in Los Angeles. Hugh calls Americans 'aliens' because when the band first arrived in the States, it was like being on another planet to them. Basically, the song belittles fake Americana.

Hugh, at the time, was also working with Robert Williams from Captain Beefheart's band on the *Nosferatu* album (See 'Solo Recordings'). The pair would often work late into the night, and this is also mentioned in the lyrics.

There are no lead or rhythm guitars on this track and Hugh plays a bass guitar as well as JJ. It's a return to the more traditional 'sinister' Stranglers songs as sung by Mr Cornwell.

'Ice'

'Ice' had its origins in a jam session and has lots going on. It's a case of The Stranglers playing around with the music in a sort of jazz-pop fusion.

JJ's lyric, which he also sings, expresses his growing fascination with Japanese culture, especially Seppuku, which is ritual suicide (more commonly known in the West as 'hara-kiri'). JJ's hero Yukio Mishima committed hara-kiri in 1970, even though the practice had been officially outlawed in 1873.

The keyboard riff is the same music used at the end of 'Shah Shah A Go Go' because the two songs had been recorded together but then separated so that they could go on different sides of the vinyl album.

'Baroque Bordello'

This song is seemingly set in a brothel, although Hugh, who wrote and sang the lyrics, has stated that the band were not frequenting that type of establishment. In reality, it's a fantasy song about a girl that Hugh knew in America.

The band all combine faultlessly on this track, and as there are hardly any overdubs, it almost sounds as if it was recorded live. It started with a riff from Hugh which only had seven notes, and try as he might, he couldn't get an eighth to fit, so it was left in 7/8 time. However, JJ is playing in 4/4 time. Dave's keyboards during the intro initiate the 'baroque' vibe – it's almost church music.

Some of the experimentation, both musically and lyrically, at this time, was taking place because the band had started taking heroin (more Hugh and JJ rather than Dave and Jet), stirring an impulse to explore different sounds and lyrical themes.

'Nuclear Device (The Wizard Of Aus)'

This showcases a Hugh vocal with political overtones. The subject matter revolves around Joh Bejelke Petersen, a Swede who had been refused entry into the United Kingdom and instead went to Australia. He entered politics and gained power in Queensland, where he installed some very strict laws about congregating and was found guilty of gerrymandering (this is the manipulation of the boundaries of an electoral constituency so that it favours one party).

The last bit of the song postulates that some of the unusual-looking animals in Australia could have resulted from mutations caused by an ancient nuclear experiment – laying the ground for the 'meninblack' theory.

'Nuclear Device' was released as a single in the UK on 3 October 1979 (United Artists BP318), with 'Yellowcake UF6' on the flip side. Not the most popular Stranglers single, reaching only number 36 in a four-week chart run, it was the first single for two and half years not to reach the top 30.

Dave puts a cheeky bit of 'Waltzing Matilda' in there at the beginning as a joke, but the band decided to keep it in.

This track is far less complex than the previous three songs as there isn't much in the way of 'layering', which makes for a less cluttered sound and less reliance on longer instrumental breaks. One of the reasons for the song's commercial failure could have been Hugh's vocals, which were more aggressive than those often found in hit material at the time.

'Shah Shah A Go Go'

Another political song from Hugh, things were kicking off in the Middle East at the time, with the main protagonists being the Shah of Iran and the Ayatollah Khomeini. The Ayatollah was living in Paris and sending cassettes (remember them?) of his teachings into Iran to stir up ill feelings against the Shah, who was living in splendour in Iran. The end result was that the Shah was ousted in 1979 and died the following year in Egypt of cancer.

At the start of the song, we have the muezzin calling the faithful to prayer. This is another experimental track with a touch of jazz-inspired music, especially towards the end. This shows itself in the interplay between Jet's drum rhythm and JJ's bass (which generally keeps the song moving at a regular pace). Dave has a four-note repeating synthesiser riff and the backing vocals have an unusual sound. All the instruments start rising in pitch a la The Beatles' 'A Day In The Life'.

'Don't Bring Harry'

This was released as an EP (United Artists STR 1) on 9 November 1979 with three other tracks: 'Wired' (taken from the *Nosferatu* album by Hugh and Robert Williams), 'Crabs' (a live version of the song from JJ's solo album *Euroman Cometh* recorded in Hemel Hempstead in 1979) and 'In The Shadows' (a live version recorded at The Hope and Anchor in 1977).

This was the only EP by the band to reach the official British EP Charts, reaching number 41 during a three-week chart residency starting on 1 December 1979.

'Wired' was written and produced by Hugh and Robert Williams, whilst 'Crabs' was written by JJ and produced by the band and Alan Winstanley.

'Don't Bring Harry' is quite a sparse-sounding song, almost semi-acoustic, with most of the chords being played on the piano rather than guitar. It's also quite slow. The music was by Hugh and the lyrics by JJ, who also sang it. It's an anti-heroin song ('Harry' being heroin) and some of the lyrics suggest being taken over by the drug, which, according to Hugh, is exactly what heroin does to you.

'Duchess'

With a vocal by Hugh, this is one of the most popular songs in the band's catalogue and a massive fan favourite. It was released as a single by United Artists (BP 308) on 8 August 1979 and reached number 14 in the UK and number 27 in Ireland. The B-side was 'Fools Rush Out'. Perhaps it might have fared better had the video not been banned by the BBC as being 'blasphemous' – it depicts the band as choirboys.

The lyrics are about a girl that Hugh knew who was a minor aristocrat (she claimed that she was a descendant of Henry VIII) and now lived in a terraced house in Chelsea. The 'Rodneys' mentioned in the song are nouveau-riche chancers with no breeding who trail aristocratic girls in order to get in with the upper class.

The song is just about one of the 'poppiest' songs The Stranglers ever recorded, and when performing it live, Dave used to delight the audiences by playing the arpeggio with one hand whilst drinking a pint of beer with the other!

'Meninblack'

Before they began work on *The Raven*, the band recorded a song called 'Two Sunspots' at Eden Studios. It was supposed to be released as a single as the gap between the albums *Black And White* and *The Raven* was so great. Having not released it in the end, they played about with it in the studio. They played it at half-speed and decided it would make a good song. Hugh played a 'cowboy' riff on the guitar and JJ wrote the lyrics. Jet added some toms and Dave played some wild keyboards. JJ's voice was again put through the harmoniser, like on 'Enough Time' on *Black And White*. In fact, when he giggles, it's reminiscent of David Bowie's 'The Laughing Gnome'.

This was the song that spelt the end of the band's working relationship with producer Martin Rushent. He arrived at the studio late one day while the band were recording this song and he didn't like what they were doing. Rushent said that if the band wanted to carry on working on the track, he would leave. They carried on and he left.

The lyrics put forward the idea that mankind is just an experiment by aliens and the earth is just a 'food farm', hence the line 'Human flesh is porky meat'. Apparently, humans taste like pork; in fact, the cannibal's name for white men translates as 'long pigs'.

The band included the track on *The Raven* as opposed to the next album as a prelude to prepare us for what was to come – a sort of teaser.

It was played at the 50th-anniversary shows at the end as the lights went up and the audience were leaving.

'Genetix'

Dave sings this. It was written by Hugh, but it's a complicated piece to play due to its odd time signature, so Dave got the job. This was Dave's turn to shine as lead vocalist in live shows. Hugh's lyrics seem to indicate that he wasn't a great fan of genetic manipulation, and having been a research biochemist, he knows what he's talking about.

It's another piece of musical experimentation. The song begins with an instantly recognisable drum riff from Jet and a seemingly atonal guitar from Hugh. 'Genetix' again shows how important instrumentation was to The Stranglers, with almost four minutes of vocal-less music in nearly five minutes and a half minutes. As an added bonus, we get a bass solo from JJ just after the halfway mark.

Other Contemporary Tracks

'Bear Cage'

The first Stranglers release of the new decade was 'Bear Cage', a single released by United Artists (BP 344) on 7 March 1980. The B-Side was 'Shah Shah A Go Go'. A 12" version was released with extended versions of both tracks and was produced by the band with Alan Winstanley. It was the first 12" single that the band released and Hugh had mixed the longer version at Air Studios with engineer Steve Churchyard.

The song grew out of a soundcheck at a gig in France. With JJ's bass riff and Hugh doing the chords, it was the first new song the band had written since *The Raven* and is The Stranglers' attempt at doing a mechanical disco song. Disco was very much in vogue and the band were influenced by robotic bands like Devo and Kraftwerk. Sadly, the single peaked at number 36 and only spent five weeks in the UK charts.

The 'GmbH' in the lyrics means 'limited company' in German and the song is about a young man living in East Germany. The bear is both the symbol of Berlin and Russia and Hugh was thinking of East Germany being surrounded by a Russian Bear (literally a bear cage).

'Fools Rush Out'

This – the B-side to 'Duchess' – was about the two managers of the band: Dai Davies and Derek Savage. They parted company after suggesting the band split up. One (Savage) wanted material things, like fame and money, whilst the other (Davies) wanted to have fun and create something musically memorable. Overall, it's a mid-tempo Stranglers song and a pretty typical one at that.

'N'Emmenes Pas Harry'

This is the French version of 'Don't Bring Harry' released as a single in France by United Artists (2C 008-82.868). The B-side was listed on the disc as 'Livin' In A Bear Cage' ('Bear Cage' with a longer title).

'Yellowcake UF6'

This is an instrumental written by Hugh. The band once walked off stage whilst doing the live TV show *Rock Goes To College* and then wrote a song called 'Social Secs' about the event. This is that song played backwards. 'Social Secs' remains unreleased.

Listening to it now, the drums sound like the B-side to Napoleon XIV's 'They're Coming To Take Me Away, Ha Haa' (1966) as it was the A-side played backwards. True eccentricity in the recording studio.

UF6 is the chemical symbol for Uranium Hexafluoride, the material from which Uranium is extracted. Yellowcake is a type of concentrated powder used in the processing of Uranium.

The Gospel According To The Meninblack (1981)

Personnel:
Hugh Cornwell (Hughinblack): guitar, vocals.
Jean-Jacques Burnel (JJinblack): bass guitar, vocals
Dave Greenfield (Daveinblack): keyboards, vocals
Jet Black (Jetinblack): drums, vocals, percussion
Recorded at Musicland Studios, Munich, Pathe Marconi Studios, Paris, Startling Studios, Berkshire, RCA Studios, Rome, Pebble Beach Sound Studio, Worthing, Eden Studios, London in May 1979 and between January and August 1980
Producer: The Stranglers
Engineers: Alan Winstanley, Steve Churchyard, Aldo Bocca, Laurence Diana
Original UK label and catalogue number: Liberty Records LBG 30313
Released: 9 February 1981 (UK)
Highest chart position: UK: 8, New Zealand: 40
Running time: 40.28
All tracks written by The Stranglers (Hugh Cornwell, Jean-Jacques Burnel, Dave Greenfield, Jet Black)

A change of label ensued for this album, as The Stranglers moved to a United Artists subsidiary – Liberty. Things appeared to be quieter for the band in 1980 and we had another long wait for an album – this time 17 months! But it was a hectic time for our heroes. After 'Bear Cage', the only other release was a non-album single, 'Who Wants The World' b/w 'The Meninblack (Waiting For 'Em)', which was a prelude to the next album.

A period of bad luck descended upon the band leading up to the *Meninblack* album. A member of the roadcrew (Alan McStravich) was carted off to hospital with a drug-induced heart attack because he took a line of Angel Dust thinking it was heroin. Kevin Sparrow, who had designed the band's logo and the cover of *Black And White*, died on Christmas day after drinking a whole bottle of whiskey and then accidentally taking a Mogadon capsule. Add to that the death of the band's tour manager Charlie Pyle, from cancer at the age of 24.

Not just that, but Sparrow's photographs, the band's songbook, a biography and the master tapes to *The Raven* went missing. A radio broadcast of a show recorded in New Jersey had some voices missing and the studio blew up! And not forgetting Hugh's arrest and the band's 'holiday' in a Nice jail! The band were arrested on 21 June in Nice and charged with 'inciting a riot'. Hugh, JJ and Jet were incarcerated in Nice jail, whilst Dave was released as he hadn't actually said anything to the crowd and therefore could not have been inciting anything. The whole, sordid story is recounted in Jet's book *Much Ado About Nothing*, which was published by The Stranglers' Information Service in February 1981 and enlarged upon and updated in his book *Seven Days In Nice*, published by Coursegood Books in 2010.

This, of course, wasn't Hugh's only trip to the cells this year. On 7 January, he was found guilty of the possession of heroin, cocaine and cannabis.

Hugh was fined £300 and sentenced to three months in Pentonville. He unsuccessfully appealed in March and was eventually released on 25 April. In the meantime, the band performed two benefit concerts with friends at The Rainbow Theatre in London, which were eventually released as a live album some years later (Please see 'Live Albums').

When it came to recording the album, the band had been working around the clock, using six different studios with different engineers (fuelled by different drugs) to get the album completed. However, it was only released a full six months after the completion of recording.

The Gospel According To The Meninblack is the band's first bona fide concept album. In a nutshell, Earth was visited by aliens in the distant past and the Biblical 'miracles' could be attributed to advanced alien technology. Coming forward in time to the present day, the 'men in black' are agents of a secret US government department sent out to question people who claim they had had an alien encounter. This concept is also looked at – in a more humorous way – by the *Men In Black* film franchise.

The album's front cover had the titles and the band logo, plus the credits of the album, in a mock Gothic script. Inside – linking the two main themes of aliens and religion – is a version of Leonardo Da Vinci's 'The Last Supper' (painted around 1495 – 1498) with a maninblack on the right. It was produced by design company Shoot That Tiger.

The band – especially Hugh – played up to the concept by referring to themselves as 'Hughinblack', 'JJinblack', etc. etc. and the band are nicknamed to this day as 'The Men in Black'. In fact, the band were approached by BBC South-West in Bristol to make a documentary for their programme *RPM*. Hugh and Jet came up with a film about the colour black and how it seemed to be associated with evilness and negativity. It received good reviews and an extension to the idea was mooted, but when the producers went to the archive to find the original tapes, they had disappeared!

The band were happy with the album, saying it was their best work and ground-breaking, as according to JJ, it was almost 'techno' before techno existed. As a consequence, the band were disheartened by its poor sales. It reached number eight in the UK charts but spent only five weeks there. This pointed to a decline in the fortunes of the band, which had started with *The Raven*.

'Waltzinblack'

Probably the most famous instrumental by the band, this is used to introduce the band at every live show. The basic tune came from JJ, which he gave to Dave to play and embellish on keyboards; in fact, there is no other instrumentation apart from the keyboards. It's a waltz in 3/4 time (hence 'Waltzinblack'). Once recorded at Pathe Marconi Studio, Hugh thought that something was missing, so they added the maniacal (forced) laughing and put the voices through the harmoniser.

It has been suggested that this should have been a single but has been used as a TV theme (Keith Floyd) and on commercials (Strepsils and Vodaphone). 'Waltzinblack' ended up on the flip side of 'La Folie' in 1982. The song was also added as a B-side to the 12" version of 'Grip '89', and the version from the Vodaphone advert was used as an extra track on the 'Long Black Veil' single in 2004.

'Just Like Nothing On Earth'

This was released as a single on Liberty Records (BP 393) on 13 March 1981, with 'Maninwhite' on the flip. Perhaps being put out so soon after the release of the album affected sales, as it was the first Stranglers single NOT to trouble the chart compilers.

Hugh's guitar part, over the frantic bass riff, is a style of music from Ghana called Highlife (not Zaire as Hugh said in *Song By Song*). It tends to be a fusion of Western jazz and African music; to put it simply, African music played with Western instruments, generally horns and guitars. And what we think is a didgeridoo at the beginning is Dave using a Wasp keyboard. This is to show communication, as the aboriginal instrument is used for communicating. Hugh's fascination with 'native' music would eventually result in the *Dreamtime* album in 1986. The Wasp keyboards (actually called the Electronic Dream Plant Wasp) eventually came in three versions. The first (1978) had a two-octave range and was in black and yellow. The Wasp Deluxe (1979) had three octaves and a wood finish and the Wasp Special (1981) had a wood finish again but in black and gold. Apart from Dave, it was notably used by Nick Rhodes from Duran Duran and Vince Clarke.

Lyrically, Hugh describes alien encounters that he read about and the title comes from the fact that many people said that their experience was 'just like nothing on earth'. He sings the word 'earth' in that unique way to denote disgust. Another interesting thing about the lyrics is that a lot of the words are alliterative, such as 'A Nip in Nippon napped a nod and knew a new nomad near the nearside window of his Mitsubishi'. Because of the tongue-twisting and fast nature of the lyrics, it took a lot of rehearsing to be able to sing it live.

'Second Coming'

Inspired by the fascination in the belief that Christ will come again, Hugh theorises that if Christ came back to earth, no one would believe Him, much like us not believing lunatics when they say they are Him. How will He look? How will He speak? All this is asked in the lyrics. It touches on the 'Meninblack' concept of alien visitation in that the miracles and visions described in The Bible could be alien intelligence and flying saucers.

The music is interesting, featuring a jangly Hugh riff and a rather funky bass line from JJ. The chorus is spoken rather than sung, and the music stopping was JJ's idea. It comes back again as a 'second coming'. There is a mantra-like chant which continues as the music fades out; this hypnotic feel is repeated in other songs on the album, such as 'Waiting For The Meninblack', 'Hallow To Our Men' and 'Manna Machine'. This was to give a quasi-religious vibe, in keeping with the album's title.

'Waiting For The Meninblack'

This tells the story of someone who has been visited in the past by the Men in Black and is looking out for them again. He is scared, and so he holds a teddy bear as a comfort. The 'vortex' sound was created by Dave setting up a waveform on his synthesiser and speeding it up. Overall, another hypnotic track with a repetitive – and seemingly discordant – chorus.

'Turn The Centuries, Turn'

A melancholy song in a minor key and another Stranglers instrumental, this was recorded in Weybridge at John Lennon's old house. By now, it belonged to Ringo Starr and you could record in every room as there were microphones set up everywhere.

JJ plays the melody on the bass and Hugh adds a countermelody by plucking the guitar. He also adds some backwards guitar, which helps achieve the overall 'unearthly' feel in the background. Meanwhile, Dave creates a 'dreamy' mood with a backdrop of synthesiser, which appears to 'shimmer', but the notes are slightly 'bent', making it sound as if it isn't quite in tune. Jet recorded a drum loop, something that would be later done on drum machines.

'Two Sunspots'

As mentioned earlier, this song was recorded in 1978 and was slowed down to become the song 'Meninblack'. The track wasn't re-recorded and the band used the original tape. It rolls along at quite a good pace.

At the time, the newspapers were printing a lot about sunspots and how they affect us, and Hugh does allude to that, although the song is actually about nipples: 'Two rough round red raw real sunspots'. The 'Men in Black' concept is subtle, but Hugh gets the message across subliminally that even on the brightest thing (i.e. the Sun), there is darkness.

'Four Horsemen'

Another reference to Nostradamus graces this track, but it's very strange in that, during the song, the guitar, bass and drums play a riff before repeating it with an added note. The next time, they add two notes and so on until they have added six extra notes to the original riff. After that, they go back to the original riff. Then, as Hugh stated in 2001, 'The verse goes all over the place, musically. Dave followed the chord line and managed to construct a melody line around all of these changes to the bass line' – but the band liked it. Furthermore, there is a rather nice and lengthy (almost two-thirds of the song) instrumental break to finish the song.

Nostradamus wrote about the Four Horsemen of the Apocalypse. The rider on the red horse is war, the black horse is famine, the pale horse is death and the white represents Jesus. In the song, they are depicted as four spaceships.

Dave sang this, not because it was difficult to play and sing, but because Hugh and JJ were of the opinion that he should sing at least one song on every album. Sadly, this didn't work out and it was the last time that Dave had a lead vocal.

'Thrown Away'

The Stranglers go 'disco' with this track, recorded at Musicland Studios in Munich, where Donna Summer had recorded all her disco classics and where Queen and the Electric Light Orchestra constructed their masterpieces.

Released as a single on 19 January 1981, it was the band's first release on the Liberty label (when United Artists was sold to EMI, the powers that be put The Stranglers, as well as Dr Feelgood and Hawkwind, on Liberty – the home of Alvin and The Chipmunks, The Bonzo Dog Doo-dah Band, Captain Beefheart, Vikki Carr and Del Shannon), with the catalogue number BP 383. It was the band's attempt at a 'Euro-disco' song and they were confident that it would be a hit. However, the single only reached number 42 in a four-week chart stay.

One of this author's personal favourites, it was the first song that the band worked on after Hugh had come out of Pentonville jail and had a week's holiday with Hazel O'Connor in Italy. JJ's lyrics are set to Hugh's melody as JJ puts himself in the shoes of our alien visitors, asserting that we have had our chances to make this world a great place to be, but we have thrown them all away. Such a sad lyric to a very upbeat song, spoken in a very low growl. Strangely, this was the only track on the album with a JJ lead vocal. Mind you, the album was arguably Hugh's brainchild, and therefore, he had most of the lyrical ideas.

It was at this point that JJ took a back seat with the lyric writing and singing. Apparently, he was never confident in his voice and his vocal contributions would also diminish on stage. After Hugh left, the band recruited a single vocalist (Paul Roberts) and JJ thought it best that, as the new vocalist, he should have a chance at interpreting all the songs. JJ tells me that he recovered his confidence after the *Norfolk Coast* album.

'Manna Machine'

This is a Hugh song which came from a studio jam and was written and recorded in a day. Aside from Hugh's guitars and Dave's keyboard wash, there isn't much music, more a collection of sounds. However, there is a drum loop by Jet, which was recorded in a similar way to Pink Floyd's loops on *The Dark Side Of The Moon*, where the band stood around the studio with pencils around which the tape would travel. A primitive form of loop, but quite effective. There is a sense of 'things to come' in the music world, as this type of music was what the 'techno' bands would be doing in a year or two. This proves that the band were way ahead of their time.

It's very atmospheric and is inspired by a book called *Manna Machine* by George Sassoon (1978). It theorised that a machine appeared in the desert, which created manna to feed the Israelites during their exodus. The machine disappeared and the book states that it could be buried in a cave in the Golan Heights. Manna was a type of food tasting of honey; it's mentioned twice in the Bible and three times in the Quran.

'Hallow To Our Men'

The album closes with another track that Hugh described as 'jazz-pop'. JJ wrote the melody, and it was nearly another instrumental, but Hugh decided to add the lyrics, which are an 'alternative' Lord's Prayer. Then, there is a beautiful melody which builds to a crescendo. At the end, there is a spaceship taking off (it had landed at the beginning of 'Just Like Nothing On Earth'). In the song, he is asking for mercy and asking to be allowed to live, even though we have failed to look after our planet properly.

It starts in 5/4 time and is a little free form, so when Hugh added the vocals, he made it sound like a 'Beatnik' poem from the 50s, with him snapping his fingers. Dave's keyboards at the beginning are slightly reminiscent of The Who's 'Baba O'Reilly'. It's a very long intro, with the vocals only coming in after two minutes and 48 seconds.

Other Contemporary Tracks

'Who Wants The World'

This is the A-side of a single released on 29 May 1980 (United Artists BP 355). The single spent four weeks in the UK charts, reaching number 39. As is quite often the case, this song was created from a bass riff by JJ, to which Hugh added the melody and lyrics. Recorded in The Church Studio in north London, just before Hugh's appeal about his jail sentence, the record company (and the band) missed out, as they didn't release it until May after his release. If it had been released while the singer had been in jail, perhaps the press exposure could have generated more sales.

Quite a jaunty and commercial song, the subject matter is a little dark and is a teaser of the 'Men in Black' concept, throwing the theory out there but not explaining it until later. According to the lyrics, an alien comes down to earth and eats both man and a flea but can't tell the difference. It even speaks to a tree. The alien is disappointed at what we have done to the planet and asks, 'who would want it?'. The last line about a 'Thursday sunrise sunset' is the alien looking back at the planet as he/she/it leaves and watches mankind destroy itself in a nuclear explosion.

'The Meninblack (Waiting For 'Em)'

The B-side to 'Who Wants The World'. It's an instrumental version of the track 'Waiting For The Meninblack', which would be included on the *Meninblack* album.

'Top Secret'

The B-side to 'Thrown Away'. Hugh's voice is so deep here that as he gets lower, his voice disappears. It's a powerful bassline from JJ and appears to have been slightly 'harmonised' (see 'Maninwhite').

Nostradamus is the subject again and Hugh writes about the fact that he (Nostradamus) writes at night. By day, he's a doctor and 'he cures all the ills of the world with his knife', but as to his predictions, he isn't believed and he dies unknown.

'Maninwhite'

The B-side of 'Just Like Nothing On Earth' was recorded in Rome. The music was recorded first, and the day after, Hugh went to Rome to see the Pope address the crowd in St Peters Square and witnessed the reaction of the crowd. The lyrics are very 'tongue-in-cheek' and suggest that the Pope has a 'hotline' to God.

The incredibly fast bass drum suggests that Jet may have used a drum machine for the first time here. It's very similar to some of the earlier Stranglers songs in terms of the pace and heavy bass, which appears to be 'harmonised' like Yes's Chris Squire on their 1978 album *Tormato*.

'Tomorrow Was The Hereafter'

This was included on the 2001 reissue of the album but was recorded much earlier – in fact, when the band were trying to get their first record deal. It was written by JJ before he joined the band, and unlike him in the early days, he sings rather than shouts. The song is a pretty basic one, with lyrics saying that we should live for today. It's very much like a sixties 'beat' song, and there is a nice, well-arranged instrumental break in the middle of the track.

'Tomorrow Was The Hereafter' was given away free with the band's fan magazine *Strangled* from The Stranglers Information Service (catalogue number SIS 001) in 1980 (see also 'Cocktail Nubiles', which was the B-side). It also appeared on *The Rarities*, a compilation released in 2002.

La Folie (1981)

Personnel:
Hugh Cornwell: guitar, lead and backing vocals.
Jean-Jacques Burnel: bass guitar, lead and backing vocals
Dave Greenfield: keyboards
Jet Black: drums, percussion
Recorded at The Manor Studio, Shipton-on-Cherwell, between August and September 1981
Producer: The Stranglers and Steve Churchyard, Tony Visconti (on 'You Hold The Key To My Love In Your Hands')
Engineer: Steve Churchyard
Original UK label and catalogue number: Liberty Records LBG 30342
Released: 9 November 1981 (UK)
Highest chart position: UK: 11 (Silver), Australia: 29, Netherlands: 13
Running time: 41.27
All tracks written by The Stranglers (Hugh Cornwell, Jean-Jacques Burnel, Dave Greenfield, Jet Black)

According to The Stranglers, *La Folie* was not a concept album but apparently looks at 'love'. The love of God ('Non Stop'), love of celebrity ('Everybody Loves You'), searching for love ('Tramp'), love of family ('Let Me Introduce You To The Family') – you get the picture. From a commercial point of view, it had to do well, and as a consequence, three singles from the album were released.

Tony Visconti was selected to mix the album as Hugh liked the way he made Bowie's voice sound. Hugh was singing more (rather than shouting, growling or speaking) and he wanted it to be heard properly. Also, the record company instructed Visconti to mix each track as though it were a single. His overall input gave the album a more commercial and polished sound.

The album was written just a month before recording because the band had a lot of material. JJ developed a lot of bass riffs, and with two instrumentals on *Meninblack*, Hugh had a lot of ideas for lyrics. In fact, he wrote the lyrics to all but two songs on the album. Also, up to now, the trademark bass of JJ was very prominent in the mix. Visconti lowered it a bit because he thought it was drowning out the voice – this was something that Hugh had been thinking about for a while. The band wrote most of the songs at Jet Black's house. He had a room where they set up the drums at one end, the keyboard at the other and guitar and bass in the middle. They were trying to recreate the way they wrote in the early days. It was very relaxed, unlike the pressure they had at Bear Shank Lodge for *Meninblack*. This was also the last album for a while that Jet played live drums in the studio, preferring to use Simmonds electronic drums in the future.

When released, the album originally performed less well than expected but received a boost when 'Golden Brown', the second single from the album, was a massive hit. As a result, *La Folie* spent 18 weeks in the charts. However, the band were looking for a loophole in their contract in order to leave EMI. Apparently, they had been told that if this album didn't do well, they could end up looking for another label. Being a band that liked to control their own destiny, they instructed their lawyers to look for the aforementioned loophole, which they eventually found.

The cover is a strange one and not one of their 'obvious' ones. It has treated photographs of the four band members (with a slight blue tinge to my eyes), the album title in red – in a rather 'fancy' script – and no band name.

'Non Stop'

According to Hugh, this was originally called 'Non Stop Nun', an alliterative title (which he likes). The term 'non stop' describes the fact that a nun's devotion is 24/7 and it also implies motion, reinforced by JJ's bass riff. It was he who came up with the classical-style riff and Dave played it on the organ so it would sound more church-like. Hugh describes the song as 'an amusing take on ecclesiastical life'. He describes how religion takes over the nun's life and that she is repressed – how does she deal with those more 'forbidden' feelings? It's quite catchy; when writing the songs, the band had the desire for a hit single in their minds. This would probably have been a hit if released a couple of years later, as it has – in this author's view – a 'New Romantic' vibe.

'Everybody Loves You When You're Dead'

The concept of 'fickleness' is to the fore here, as people's views on someone sometimes change when they die. The song was triggered (no pun intended) by the assassination of John Lennon and the fact that people only started saying how truly great he was after his death. It also alludes to the press and the fact that they can be in your corner at one time and then turn on you. There's a reference in the song to 'the sun' – not just the star, but to the newspaper. Overall, it is a Hugh song that returns to the 'Devo' sound that had cropped up a few times in previous albums.

'Tramp'

The band wanted this track to be the follow-up to 'Golden Brown', but JJ talked them out of it. It was Hugh's song, both musically and lyrically, and even the record company wanted to release it as a single to capitalise on the success of the previous massive smash. Hugh says that this song is a bit autobiographical, detailing a mythical tramp with wanderlust. Hugh used to dress as a tramp in the very early days of the band. The 'trademark' bass sound is to the fore here. Make the most of it, as this was to become less important to the sound of the band in subsequent albums.

'Let Me Introduce You To The Family'

The A-side of a single released on 7 November 1981 (two days before the album) on Liberty Records (BP405). It reached number 42 in the UK charts during a three-week chart run. The flip side was 'Vietnamerica'. There are Mafia overtones and the cover of the single showed a family around the table (which could almost have been a still from *The Godfather*) with Tommy guns as a background. The song was inspired by a pupil who had been taught by Hugh. They were very close, which made Hugh a bit envious as he didn't have the same familial closeness. Guitar adorns this disco-esque commercial track, with a long bass intro which smacks of 'No More Heroes'.

'Ain't Nothin' To It'

The lyrics on 'Ain't Nothin' To It' are credited to Milton 'Mezz' Mezzrow (1899 – 1972), an American jazz clarinettist and saxophonist. He invented his own language called 'jive talk'. This was so he could talk to his customers in slang (as well as forming the first band in New York with both black and white musicians; he was also a drug dealer). Hugh read his autobiography (*Really The Blues*) and selected a number of expressions which he turned into lyrics. Mr. Cornwell was using what he called a 'Razor' guitar, which enabled him to get higher notes than on other guitars. This was the only album he used it on.

'The Man They Love To Hate'

This is another song where the 'Razor' guitar is to the fore, and Hugh seems to be enjoying playing it. Hugh gave JJ the title for him to put a lyric to and JJ duly obliged. At the time, the TV show *Dallas* was a big hit, and the character JR Ewing was the man that everyone loved to hate. JJ also used, as an analogy, the fact that he'd just split up from a girl. In a way, it's about getting pleasure from hating someone. And, given the roastings that The Stranglers usually got in the press, it could almost be their theme song. There are also references to his parents and the love-hate relationship the band had with London. It's quite a dark lyric that JJ delivers like a poem, but the music carries it along nicely, with a driving beat and quite heavy drumming. The 'echo' on the bass was created by JJ playing his bass through a delay line – a device he used on 'Non Stop'.

The band enjoyed playing this one live, and when they did a Radio 1 session to promote *La Folie*, this was the only track from the album they played.

Depending on where you look, the song is labelled as 'The Man …' or 'The Men …'. In a conversation in 2023, JJ assured me that it should be 'The Man …'.

'Pin Up'

Lyrically, this song is straightforward, as images of women on a wall give the viewer lustful thoughts. Dave's keyboards have an 'aquatic' sound. This was probably created by the use of auto-pan, where you take the sound and process it so that it floats from speaker to speaker. JJ also use the delay on the bass again. And there appears not to be a lot of guitar and a 'disco' beat on the drums. This is a prime example of Visconti following the record company's directive of mixing the track as though it could be a single.

'It Only Takes Two To Tango'

This is not to be confused with Richard Myhill's 1978 hit 'It Takes Two To Tango'. The vocals here sound reminiscent of The Beach Boys, with both JJ and Hugh sharing lead vocals for the first and last time on a track. It's rather apt when you consider the title and it must have taken their voices to the very top of their respective ranges. Therefore, it was rarely performed live.

Inspired by The Cold War, which was still hanging over us all (there is an image of Presidents Reagan and Brezhnev dancing on the album's cover), Hugh started to think about other things where you need two, hence the reference to Adam and Eve – 'it only took two in ancient history/to get to the top of the monkey tree'.

'Golden Brown'

Arguably, this is the band's most famous number, but strangely, it's not representative of their output. It's one of only two Stranglers singles to spend more than ten weeks in the charts with 12. The other was 'Peaches' with 14. The single had a very non-descript cover, with just the band logo and song title in gold on a plain brown background. 'Love 30' was the flip side. The single was released in the UK on Liberty Records (BP 407) on 11 January 1982 (although some stockists had it for sale before Christmas 1981) and it reached number two in the UK, held off the top by 'The Lion Sleeps Tonight' by Tight Fit and 'A Town Called Malice' by The Jam. It sold over 600,000 copies, earning a platinum disc. It was even 'Diddy' David Hamilton's 'Record of the Week' on BBC Radio 2. In 2012, Radio 2 had a listener's poll regarding the favourite singles to have peaked at number two. 'Golden Brown' came fifth. It did well around the world, reaching number ten in Australia, number seven in Belgium, number 73 in France, number 63 in Germany, number three in Ireland, number seven in Poland, and in the Netherlands, where they had two charts (could it have been 'double Dutch'?), it reached number eight and ten. There have been a number of reasons why it didn't get to the top of the UK charts. One was that the sales of 'A Town Called Malice' included both 7" and 12". Secondly, Hugh said in 2017 that JJ told a journalist the song was about heroin, which resulted in everybody dropping the song from their playlists. Also, EMI didn't press enough copies to satisfy demand, which also affected sales.

The song came from a piece of music that Dave had been tinkering with for a while but couldn't find an outlet. Hugh heard him playing it at Jet's house and said that they shouldn't add anything to it and treat it as a piece of music by itself. He then sat down, and in about ten minutes, he had the lyrics. Jet loved the song and said it would be a smash, but JJ wasn't impressed. In fact, he didn't play on the original track as Dave played the root notes on keyboards. However, when played live, it's JJ playing them on the bass.

The tempo of the song is unusual, as in the instrumental parts, there are three bars of 3/4 followed by one bar of 4/4. Effectively, it becomes 13/8. When the vocals come in, it's a strict 3/4. The main keyboard is the harpsichord, which gives the song a sound very much rooted in the 1700s when harpsichords were all the rage and the waltz reigned supreme. Hugh's guitar solo is a highlight of the record, and even more so live; these days, when Baz Warne plays it, there is a round of applause every time. It is said that Hugh was never able to get it correct – even on the album, there are a couple of takes edited together.

The lyrics can be looked at in two ways. Firstly, it's about a Mediterranean woman with golden brown skin that Hugh knew, and secondly, it was about heroin and how it makes you feel.

'How To Find True Love And Happiness In The Present Day'

This has the longest title (without brackets) of any Stranglers track. The melody came from JJ and the lyrics (which are more or less spoken) from Hugh. The Stranglers Information Service issued a CD of rare recordings by the band, and one song is called 'Gone Are Those Days'. This is the same song but with different lyrics. This features a lovely melody – even though the guitar is rather sparse – similar to 'Pin Up', with Jet using a proper drum kit. The lyrics are about some people Hugh knew. He refers to the things they love and what they thought was missing in their lives. Sadly, looking back at the song in 2001, Hugh couldn't remember who any of the people were.

'La Folie'

The band left the title track and the album's longest song at over six minutes to the end. It was the third and last single taken from the album and was released by Liberty Records (BP 410) on 20 April 1982. The band wanted 'Tramp' as the last single but were eventually persuaded by JJ to go for 'La Folie' instead. It spent just three weeks in the UK chart and only reached number 47. Apparently, Hugh had a 'told you so' look on his face for weeks afterwards.

It is a slow ballad with lush background instrumentation and superb guitar sounds. It has links with the theme of love; the band suggest that 'love' is the ultimate folly. 'La Folie' translates as 'The madness'. It was decided that the song be recorded in French, something agreed by both JJ and Hugh. JJ thought it would be a hit because no one had recorded a British hit in French before. Obviously, he hadn't heard of 'Dominique', a 1963 hit by The Singing Nun, which topped the charts in seven countries (including the US) and was a top 20 hit in nine others. Sadly, 'La Folie' failed to emulate 'Dominique's success. When translated, we find that 'La Folie' is based on the true story of a Japanese student – Issei Sagawa – who was so in love with his girlfriend that he didn't want anyone else to have her, so he killed her and then ate her. This was JJ's obsession with cannibalism resurfacing.

Other Contemporary Tracks

'Cruel Garden'

This was the B-side of 'Strange Little Girl'. Hugh wanted to play acoustic guitar on this track, on which he wanted to sound like the guitar maestro Django Reinhardt. Dave played a keyboard effect which sounded like a violin and the end result resembles a duet between Reinhardt and Stephane Grappelli. To give it an even more authentic and 'jazzy' vibe, Jet used brushes instead of sticks. Hugh had an acoustic guitar specially made for him by the Kincade brothers in Bristol (yes, it was black), which he used on this track. JJ also got a Spanish guitar and an acoustic bass.

The lyrics, which were written in about five minutes, are a different take on the track 'Down In The Sewer'. In this song, the sewer is now a garden – a cruel one. The line 'Better get out of the woods today' refers to the children's song 'Teddy Bear's Picnic'.

'Cocktail Nubiles'

This is a longer and more pornographic version – if that were possible – of 'Bring On The Nubiles', recorded during the *Meninblack* sessions and complete with studio chat – basically, the band are messing about. It swings to the music of Frank Sinatra's 'Young At Heart'. It was released as the B-side to 'Tomorrow Was The Hereafter', a single issued exclusively by The Stranglers Information Service to the fan club members. The lyrics are by The Stranglers and the music, i.e. 'Young At Heart', is by Johnny Richards (1911 – 1968) and Carolyn Leigh (1926 – 1983).

'Vietnamerica'

This was the B-side to 'Let Me Introduce You To The Family', another play on words from Hugh – Vietnam and America – which he wrote after seeing the film 'Apocalypse Now'. The Vietnam War ended in 1975 with the Americans on the losing side – the lyrics make this clear: 'Omnipotent gods have burnt their hands'.

The music came from a bass riff by JJ, with the guitar chords and melody from Hugh. It sounds very much like The Doors. Dave's keyboard style has been likened to The Doors many times; although Dave claimed that he wasn't a fan of the American band, he only knew of them because of their UK hits. In fact, both JJ and Hugh were Doors fans.

'Love 30'

This was the B-side to Golden Brown. This instrumental came from a jam between JJ and Jet. They playfully added some samples of tennis umpires and tennis balls to the music, which strangely had little input from Dave. The band cheekily sent it to the BBC in the vain hope that they would use the song as the theme for the Wimbledon tennis championships. Auntie turned it down flat, preferring to keep with the traditional theme ('Light And Tuneful', written by Keith Mansfield and recorded by TV Sounds Unlimited).

'You Hold The Key To My Love In Your Hands'

Not your usual Stranglers fare, this has a totally different sound from the rest of the album, which was probably why it wasn't included on the disc. A very jokey lyric about a woman holding a man's penis is what you will be greeted with here. This track first appeared on the 1999 compilation *Hits And Heroes* and then again on the 2001 reissue of *La Folie.*

'Strange Little Girl'

The band signed off from EMI with this single – and a greatest hits album with the worst cover in the history of rock music (more about which later). In the negotiations with their record company, The Stranglers agreed to give EMI one more single, as well as the aforementioned Greatest Hits album. For the single, they decided to rework a song they'd demoed in 1974 (and which was incidentally turned down by EMI, amongst others). 'Strange Little Girl' was written by Hugh with Swedish musician Hans Warmling, who had been a bandmate of Hugh's in Johnny Sox, and was in The Stranglers from the inception to early 1975. When he left, he cited that he didn't want to play other people's songs (the band were still playing covers at the time). Because it was a slow, wistful song, the band thought it might be bought by those who liked 'Golden Brown' so that they could pull back some of their momentum after the failure of the 'La Folie' single.

The song's lyrics were changed from the original 1974 version and it's about the same girl Hugh wrote about in the song 'Sometimes', the one he slapped. She owned horses which were stabled some distance away, so the lyrics told us about a strange little girl who didn't like living in the town and went into the country where she was happier.

'Strange Little Girl' was in the live set from the start of The Stranglers' story, but when the band started to be lumped in with the 'punk' movement, it was dropped from the set, as it probably wouldn't have been liked by the audiences at that particular stage in the band's career.

The single was released on 9 July 1982 on Liberty (BP 412), with 'Cruel Garden' on the flip side. It returned The Stranglers to the top ten in the UK, reaching, as it did, number seven during a nine-week run. It also reached number seven in Ireland and number eight in Poland.

Interestingly, the little girl on the sleeve of the single is Jet Black's daughter Charlotte.

Feline (1983)

Personnel:
Hugh Cornwell: guitar, vocals.
Jean-Jacques Burnel: bass guitar, vocals
Dave Greenfield: keyboards
Jet Black: drums, percussion
Additional personnel:
Anna Von Stern: backing vocals (on 'Paradise')
France Lhermitte: backing vocals (on 'Paradise')
Recorded at ICP Studios, Brussels, in September 1982
Producer: The Stranglers and Steve Churchyard
Engineer: Steve Churchyard
Original UK label and catalogue number: Epic Records EPC 25237
Released: 22 January 1983 (UK)
Highest chart position: UK: 4 (Silver), Canada: 88, Germany: 52, Netherlands: 39, Norway: 16, New Zealand: 18
Running time: 38.31
All tracks written by The Stranglers (Hugh Cornwell, Jean-Jacques Burnel, Dave Greenfield, Jet Black)

Having managed to extricate themselves from their EMI contract, after the release of the single 'Strange Little Girl' and the compilation album *The Collection 1977 – 1982* (with the worst album cover ever), the band seemed ready to sign to Richard Branson's Virgin label, but at the last minute, CBS came up with a better offer, which the band's accountants advised them to accept for financial reasons. Unfortunately, in Hugh's opinion, this was not the best move, as he felt that Virgin would have had a better working relationship. The band were now on the same label as the likes of Michael Jackson and the label would work much harder for those artists than The Stranglers. But they signed to CBS/Epic in March 1982.

1982 had proved to be a very good year for the band. The last three singles released for their former label had a more gentle sound and were of a mellower nature than anything their audience had been previously accustomed to. So, when *Feline* was released, it perhaps shouldn't have been such a surprise to both fans and critics alike that there was such a perceived musical shift. Hugh and JJ's acquisition of acoustic guitars from a now world-renowned guitar maker (Kinkade's) in Bristol helped shape *Feline* into becoming possibly the nearest thing to an 'unplugged' studio album the band had yet made, although Jet was now using more electronic drums and Dave more synthesisers. The band thought it would make an interesting paradox by having acoustic guitars with electronic drums and keyboards, which were more in keeping with European music at the time, merging the traditional sounds of the acoustic guitar with the electronic sounds of the future. Gone were the powerful, sinister, throbbing melodies of their New Wave sound and in came an extraordinary and, at that time, a hitherto unheard mix of acoustic and electronic delights. Having said that, from the black cat on the sleeve (back to the 'obvious' sleeve designs again – a black cover with the outline of a lioness or panther) to the underlying melodies of the record, underpinned by that unmistakable growling bass, the band still managed to convey their dark, menacing, moody, slightly unsettling and quietly threatening no-nonsense persona.

Much of *Feline* was written at Jet's house – a disused railway station in Gloucestershire – and as soon as the band were free from the shackles of EMI, Epic arranged for them to decamp to ICP Studios in Brussels for all of September 1982 to record it. The band produced the album with Steve Churchyard, and Tony Visconti again mixed it. Being mainly produced by the band meant that some of the songs didn't have the necessary polish.

An incident during the recording of this album was the beginning of the end of Hugh's tenure with the band. He and Jet had been working on one of the songs until the early hours of the morning. When JJ and Dave arrived the next day, they listened to the work, put the tape in an envelope and stuck it on the door with a note saying, 'This is shit'. Admittedly, the bassist and keyboard player were extremely drunk at the time. This incensed both Hugh and Jet, and Hugh actually packed his bags, saying that he couldn't work with people like that (those who didn't respect his work). Ready to fly home, he received calls from both JJ and Dave apologising profusely. He was not best pleased, however.

Upon release, the band gained another silver disc as it was a top-five hit and spent 11 weeks on the charts. But more importantly, the album – probably because of its more 'European' sound – did well across the continent and opened up mainland Europe for them. The initial copies of the album came with a free, one-sided seven-inch single of the track 'Aural Sculpture Manifesto' as a teaser for the next album.

'Midnight Summer Dream'

The title came from a girlfriend of Hugh's misreading a poster advertising *A Midsummer Night's Dream*. The lyrics (written by Hugh) allude to a conversation he may or may not have had with a friend of Jet's called George. It took place in the early hours when Hugh was tripping and is about the fact that people don't let on what is inside their heads. By the end of the song, Hugh has become very wise and ready to pass his wisdom on. Furthermore, the wisdom comes from maturity; the band were no longer rebels and were now part of the musical establishment which pleased Hugh, although other members of the band may not have been so happy about it. On the album, the lyric is spoken rather than sung, whilst on the single version, to make it more commercial, it's more sung than spoken. The melody was created by JJ whilst rehearsing and they translated it to keyboards to give a 'mesmerising' sound. Meanwhile, his bass part, although notable, is rather low in the mix.

'Midnight Summer Dream' was the second single from the album, released on 26 February 1983 on Epic Records (EPCA 3167) in both 7" and 12" versions, with 'Vladimir And Olga' on the B-side. It reached number 35 in the UK charts in a four-week chart residency, number 24 in Ireland and number one in Poland. The 7" version – the album track – was just over six and a half minutes in length, but the 12" version was four minutes longer.

A live version of this song, recorded on 29 April 1975 at Paris Le Zenith, was released as a B-side to the 12" version of 'Nice In Nice' in 1986.

'It's A Small World'

Put together by JJ and Hugh whilst smoking heroin, Hugh came up with the guitar parts and lyrics while JJ contributed a very odd bass line. It's a sort of stripped-down track, with the chorus being musically dominated by Spanish guitar. Jet's Simmons electric drums are obvious.

The lyric 'the valley of the blind' refers to the old phrase 'the blind leading the blind', meaning that you can't see what's going to happen, and the clock reference appears to signify that time will reveal all. Hugh was into cryptic crosswords at the time, hence the words 'the crossword's final clue'. There's also an allusion to the fact that Hugh thought that someone could have left the band at some point, as some of the band members were still insecure. He also manages to fit in another reference to Nostradamus with 'the truth being buried'. When Nostradamus's grave was excavated, there was more information about his work buried with him.

'Ships That Pass In The Night'

'Ships That Pass In The Night' is another song written by JJ and Hugh whilst under the influence of heroin. The original idea came from one of JJ's trademark bass lines. Hugh wrote the rest, with Dave adding a trumpet sound on the keys. Hugh supplies some 'jazzy' Spanish guitar, too. It's a simple chord progression that builds before settling into a jaunty melody. The lyrics are not just about women but anything you can cling to for security – like a religion or a political party's promises – and keeping the lights burning so that you don't collide in the dark. The band were travelling a lot at the time, and therefore, the members were unable to attain a deep relationship with anyone.

'European Female (In Celebration Of)'

JJ was seemingly obsessed with all things European at this time; his first solo album *Euroman Cometh*, released in 1979, had made the top 40 albums in the UK. He'd already recorded 'Don't Bring Harry' in French, and, of course, there was 'La Folie', but 'European Female' was sung by him in English. JJ's girlfriend at the time was the actress Anna Von Stern, who was part of Parisian society, and this song is mainly about her. The line about 'No emotion on her face' probably alludes to the fact that she kept herself to herself and didn't give away her thoughts.

Although JJ played the Spanish guitar exceedingly well, it's Hugh who plays it on this song. He fits it around JJ's bass line and then Dave adds a laid-back, gentle keyboard sound. The two frontmen also harmonise in the chorus, which adds another dimension to the music because in the canon of The Stranglers, harmonies are used sparingly but effectively. JJ's lead vocal is in a similar style to his vocal on 'Don't Bring Harry'.

'European Female' was the band's first single on Epic (EPCA 2893), released on 21 December 1982, with 'Savage Breast' on the flip. It spent six weeks in the UK charts, peaking at number nine, which is also the highest placing it achieved in the Irish chart. It also reached number 19 in Poland.

A live version of this song, recorded on 29 April 1975 at Paris Le Zenith, was released as a B-side to the 12" version of 'Nice In Nice' in 1986.

'Let's Tango In Paris'

Another play on words from Hugh, with him using the title of the 1973 film *Last Tango In Paris*. The song was written and recorded quickly and originated from a bass line in waltz time. Hugh wrote all the lyrics. It's quite a romantic song, exemplified by the opening lines 'Sentimental through the night/Sharing secret candlelight', and Hugh's delivery is much softer than previously. This is because the album is more acoustic and improvements in live technology meant that he could now hear himself singing. There are also some nice harmonies towards the end.

'Paradise'

Hugh wrote the music to this one and asked JJ to supply a lyric, which he wrote whilst on holiday with Anna Von Stern in Seychelles. On his return, the music for the track had been recorded, but in a much higher key than he expected, and therefore, he had a lot of problems singing it. We have a slight reggae vibe going on here, too, which makes it a better song as it distracts you from the problems that JJ was having in singing it at such a high pitch. The lyrics work on two levels. Firstly, there was the influence of the holiday location. JJ and Anna were in a luxury hotel, but just down the road was abject poverty. The locals were living in a paradise, but their lives were hardly that. Secondly, JJ could have been alluding to his relationship with Anna being less than 'heavenly'. In fact, he returned from the holiday early.

'Paradise' was released as a single in July 1983 on Epic Records (EPCA 3387) on both 7" (with 'Pawsher' on the flip) and 12" (with 'Pawsher' and 'Permission' on the flip) vinyl. It was The Stranglers' lowest-charting single so far, reaching only number 48 in a three-week chart stay in the UK and number 19 in Poland.

'All Roads Lead To Rome'

Inspired by Hugh's trips between London and New York to see his then-girlfriend, this was the last song to be written for the album and Hugh wrote the lyrics just after getting off the plane from New York. The music had been put together by JJ and Dave. Still jet-lagged upon his return to the UK, the images of New York were still uppermost in Hugh's mind, hence the straight streets, skyscrapers ('steel fingers clawing at the sky') and taxis ('yellow chariots'). The reference to eyes changing colour comes from his girlfriend's tendency to wear different colours of contact lenses. The song is spoken by Hugh rather than sung, but JJ sings in the background to add some melody. There's a synthesiser hook similar to Kraftwerk, with the bass playing a rhythm very much in a 1980s style and Jet using electronic drums on a whole song for the first time.

'Blue Sister'

The genesis of this track is unusual in that the band were in the studio but not really recording anything. They were scheduled to appear on *Top Of The Pops,* and in those days, the artists had to re-record the music on the singles and then mime to them as though they were playing live. Most artists cheated by either supplying the original, or a version with the lead vocal removed, so that the singer could perform live, but they had to pay a bit of lip service to the rule by going into the studio.

On this occasion, Dave was playing around on the keyboard and came up with a repeating echo sound, which Hugh thought they could turn into a song – 'Blue Sister' was born. The lyrics were about Dave's relationship with his girlfriend. The keyboard player had now joined JJ and Hugh in taking cocaine and heroin and, as a consequence, his behaviour was concerning his girlfriend. 'Your lover's been taken away by some friends' could mean JJ, Hugh and drugs, and there's a play on the word 'lines', meaning lines of cocaine. Hugh said in 2001 that the lyrics were meant to reassure the girl that Dave still cared about her.

Generally regarded as the weakest track on the album, Jet said in 1996 that he hated it and it was his least favourite Stranglers track of all time.

'Never Say Goodbye'

'Never Say Goodbye' is a song that Hugh wrote and brought to the band as an almost complete work, and consequently, the rest of the band didn't have a lot of input. Lyrically, it mentions two people close to the band who had died. 'Black friend of the night' is Dagenham Dave and 'White friend of the day' is Charlie Pyle, the band's former tour manager who had succumbed to cancer. Furthermore, when Hugh sings, 'Like lovers in the past/They swim and surface in our memories', he's talking about the mind's tendency to conjure images of a person from the past. It's a rather dark ballad, with Spanish guitar to the fore again.

Other Contemporary Tracks

'Savage Breast'

The B-side to 'European Female', this Hugh-written song should arguably have been included on the album (there was certainly room). Hugh tries to do his version of a David Bowie vocal, and there is a keyboard sound akin to 'Vietnamerica'. Jet's drums are obviously electronic here.

'Pawsher'

This is a weird, experimental and psychedelic little ditty developed during a jam session and JJ supplied the title. Released as a B-side on the 7" version of 'Paradise', it's very 'New Romantic' in style, with the title – the only lyric – being sung over and over. The track was recorded in New York in April 1983.

'Permission'

This was released as one of the B-sides to the 12" version of 'Paradise'. That's three tracks on the same single, all with one-word titles beginning with 'P'. There is some excellent bass from JJ in an authentic reggae style on this one, probably the closest the band ever got to authentic Caribbean-style reggae, in terms of overall arrangement. This was recorded in June 1983 in London.

The lyrics refer to the CRS police in France. The CRS (Compagnies Republicaines de Securite) are a heavy-handed police unit used for crowd control. The title 'Permission' alludes to the permission required from those higher up before the deployment of CRS. 'The presence on the corner' is a reference to the fact that they hang around on street corners waiting for their instructions, and when they have acted, they 'fade away like summer rain'. The CRS was the unit used in the contretemps the band had at Nice University.

'Vladimir And Olga'

The first instalment of the 'Vladimir' saga was released as the B-side to 'Midnight Summer Dream'. JJ came up with the music and Hugh the lyrics. For this particular track, JJ and Dave sent a tape with the bass and keyboards (some sounding not unlike the Russian instrument, the balalaika) on it to Hugh, who went with Jet into Crescent Studios in Bath to finish it off.

In this first episode, Vladimir and his family go on holiday to Odessa, but on the way, he eats some bread laced with drugs and trips or, as it is described in the lyrics, suffers 'bread mould madness'. The lyrics have a slight echo on them when the drug takes effect to denote Vladimir's trip and then he lapses into manic laughter. The full title of the song is '(The Strange Circumstances Which Lead To) Vladimir And Olga (Requesting Rehabilitation In a Siberian Health Resort As A Result Of Stress In Furthering The People's Policies)', which holds the record for the longest Stranglers song title.

'Aural Sculpture Manifesto'

This track was released as a free one-sided 7" vinyl disc with the initial copies of *Feline* to give a taster for the next album, which had already been named *Aural Sculpture*. Another 'off the wall' track, Hugh reads out the manifesto (with weird keyboard noises creeping in), which bemoans the fact that there is no real songwriting anymore. He introduces Dave, who, with his voice edited so that there are seemingly no pauses between words, describes the electronica that is causing the death of songwriting. After Hugh's final words, we have an electronic fanfare. This track replaced 'Waltzinblack' as the intro to the band's live shows during the *Feline* and *Aural Sculpture* tours in 1983 and 1985.

Aural Sculpture (1984)

Personnel:
Hugh Cornwell: guitar, vocals.
Jean-Jacques Burnel: bass guitar, vocals
Dave Greenfield: keyboards
Jet Black: percussion
Additional personnel:
Tim Whitehead: saxophone (on 'Ice Queen', 'Punch & Judy' and 'Mad Hatter')
Paul Spong: trumpet (on 'Ice Queen', 'Punch & Judy' and 'Mad Hatter')
Paul Nieman: trombone (on 'Ice Queen', 'Punch & Judy' and 'Mad Hatter')
George Chandler: backing vocals (on 'Let Me Down Easy', No Mercy' and 'Mad Hatter')
Jimmy Chambers: backing vocals (on 'Let Me Down Easy', No Mercy' and 'Mad Hatter')
Tony Jackson: backing vocals (on 'Let Me Down Easy', No Mercy' and 'Mad Hatter')
Candide: female voice (on 'Spain')
Recorded at ICP Studios, Brussels, in 1984
Producer: The Stranglers and Laurie Latham
Engineer: Laurie Latham, Christian 'Djoum' Ramon, Erwin Autrique
Original UK label and catalogue number: Epic Records EPC 26220
Released: 5 November 1984 (UK)
Highest chart position: UK: 14 (Silver), Australia: 38, Canada: 35, Germany: 17, Netherlands: 31, Norway: 16, New Zealand: 13, Sweden: 37
Running time: 43.10
All tracks written by The Stranglers (Hugh Cornwell, Jean-Jacques Burnel, Dave Greenfield, Jet Black)

The record company originally rejected the *Aural Sculpture* album and the band had to return to the studio in June and July 1984 to re-record some numbers and write new ones. Only four songs from the initial sessions in February and March – 'Skin Deep', 'North Winds', 'Punch & Judy' and 'Souls' – made it to the finished album.

The band used brass on the album for the first time. Dave Greenfield thought that, although he could reproduce the sounds of brass instruments on his keyboards, he could not capture the breathy delivery, which you can only get from live instrumentation. The three-man brass section was also used in live shows until Hugh's departure from the band. The *Aural Sculpture* theme was about music not being 'organic' anymore – hence the use of brass – but strangely, Jet's drums are all electronic.

They also used some backing vocalists to add some soulfulness that Hugh and JJ's harmonising couldn't quite generate. The three singers had toured for a while with The James Last Orchestra. George Chandler had been a member of hit disco bands Gonzalez and The Olympic Runners and went on to form London Beat. In 1986, he recorded a single for the Burnley Building Society called 'The Best Things (Begin With B)'. This was given away to customers of said society. It was written by The Troggs' Ronnie Bond and an advertising copywriter by the name of Salman Rushdie (whatever happened to him?).

Also featured on the track, which was extensively used in a TV commercial, was Clare Torry, who had been a vocalist on Pink Floyd's *Dark Side Of The Moon*.

Furthermore, this new album introduced us to new producer Laurie Latham, who had produced the successful *No Parlez* for Paul Young as Steve Churchyard went off to America. After the first batch of songs was recorded and rejected, the record company wanted to bring in an outside producer as they were unhappy with the initial production. Latham was the third choice after Marvin Gaye and Eddy Grant. His influence made the album one of the most 'poppy' albums the band recorded. It's a million miles away from the band that had given us some of the 'controversial' songs that they recorded just seven years earlier.

The album broke the band in Australia and cemented them in France and Germany. In the UK, it still managed to be awarded a silver disc, but it stalled at number 14 and stayed in the charts for ten weeks. The album was also launched in The Belfry in the West End. There, the guests listened to the album and were able to view an exhibition of artwork inspired by the album and its themes.

The cover was one of those 'not subtle' ones, with a sculpture of an ear (by John King, High's brother-in-law). The photoshoot had taken place the previous February in Trafalgar Square. Although it looked pretty sturdy and was ten feet tall, it was, in fact, made of polystyrene, and people were having their pictures taken with it.

In keeping with Dave's liking for remaining up to date with technology, the cassette version of the album contained a computer program called 'Aural Quest' for the ZX Spectrum computers. It was introduced by Dave and was an adventure game where you, acting as the band's tour manager, had to travel to Nice, New York, Stockholm, Tokyo and Brisbane to collect the payments for The Stranglers' tour. Then, you had to find and bring back four parts of a statue of an ear that the band were using on stage. The game was authored by Mike Turner, who was a school friend of Dave's and was best man at his wedding.

The band toured the album, during which there was more tension between Hugh and JJ, and in the months before the album's release, JJ and Dave released their own album *Fire And Water* (Epic 25707). It spent five weeks in the charts, reaching number 40.

But finally, proper respect and acclaim came on 5 May 1983 when, at the Grosvenor House Hotel in London, 'Golden Brown' was named 'The Most Performed Work of 1982' at the 28th annual Ivor Novello Music Awards.

'Ice Queen'

The first of three songs on the album with brass. It was Laurie Latham's idea to use brass and he brought in the musicians he had used on Paul Young's *No Parlez* album. In fact, they worked on the songs separately from The Stranglers after the songs had been recorded.

The 'Ice Queen' in question is Hugh's American girlfriend (see 'Midnight Summer Dream'). The couple had just spit up after being engaged and Hugh thought she seemed unemotional. He likens her to a playing card as he suggests that women have unreadable expressions, in other words, a 'poker' face. The line, 'One day I'd win and the next I'd lose', infers that the relationship was a bit turbulent. However, she did get Hugh off heroin, so it wasn't all bad.

'Skin Deep'

This is the A-side of the first single taken from the album, released on 25 September 1984 on Epic Records (EPCA 4738). It reached number 15 in the UK charts, spending seven weeks on the listings. It did well overseas, too, reaching number 11 in Ireland and Australia, number 17 in Belgium, number 19 in New Zealand and number 21 in the Netherlands. It was released in two formats: a 7" version, with 'Here And There' on the B-side, and a 12" version, with an extended cut of 'Skin Deep' (seven minutes and 21 seconds as opposed to three minutes and 55). The B-side again had 'Here And There', but also 'Vladimir And The Beast (Part III)'.

Hugh wrote the lyrics to 'Skin Deep', and again, his American girlfriend was part of the inspiration. With the old adage that beauty is only skin deep in mind, Hugh was suggesting that she was very beautiful on the surface but could be different when you look beyond that. The melody came from JJ and Dave plays a keyboard part, alternating between a major chord and a seventh, that he was unsure about. After some heated discussion between Dave on one side and Hugh and JJ on the other, he decided to try it and he later conceded that it worked.

For the 12" remix, Latham added some synthesised brass, which was used when played live. It's not a bad track to dance to, either.

'Let Me Down Easy'

This was the A-side to the third single from the album. It was released on 16 February 1985 on Epic Records (EPCA 6045) and reached number 48 in a four-week chart run. The single appeared not to chart anywhere else. The 7" version had 'Achilles Heel' on the flip, whereas the 12" version had 'Achilles Heel' and the instrumental 'Place De Victoires' on the flip, along with a limited-edition poster.

It's quite a soulful song and is the first to use the backing singers brought in by producer Laurie Latham, and yes, you've guessed – they were the same backing singers he used with Paul Young. This is a particularly personal song to JJ as it was written as a tribute to his father Roger, who had just passed away. Despite the personal nature, it was actually Hugh who wrote the lyrics from JJ's bass line. Hugh said in 2001 that he was imagining what it could be like when you die. Despite the subject matter, it features an upbeat melody with a nice run from Dave, which almost sounds like a church organ.

'No Mercy'

This was the second single from the album, released on 19 November 1984 on Epic (EPCA 4921) with 'In One Door' on the B-side. It spent seven weeks on the UK charts, climbing to number 37. It was released in multiple formats: 7", 12", an 'ear' shaped picture disc and a gatefold sleeve EP. In other territories, the single reached number eight in Belgium, number 28 in Germany, number 32 in the Netherlands, number 88 in Canada and number 90 in Australia.

This is a very strong song that influenced author Dave Buckley to name his authorised biography of the band after this track in 1997. JJ's bass is quite high up in the mix on this track, but it was all Hugh's idea, both music and lyrics. He'd recorded a demo of it in his own studio on an eight-track tape. Hugh was just commenting on life in general, almost like an old blues song telling us how tough life can be. Overall, it is another 'pop' song with a terrific beat and an excellent opening guitar riff, which is repeated throughout the track.

'North Winds'

The first half of the vinyl album ends with the only JJ-sung track. He wrote the lyrics based on a guitar riff given to him by Hugh. The lyrics form a sort of protest song, as there are references to wars, weapons, the creation of Israel out of Palestine and even religion. Compared to the preceding tracks, it's rather downbeat, with the lyrics being especially bleak. JJ's voice is particularly good on 'North Winds', being a bit doom-laden. The title is a reference to the harsh winds of Northern Europe. The piano intro is especially haunting, setting the scene for the song.

'Uptown'

Another JJ bass riff-inspired song in which Hugh wrote the lyrics. In fact, in 2001, Hugh stated that only 'North Winds', 'Punch & Judy', 'Ice Queen', 'Skin Deep', 'Let Me Down Easy' and 'Uptown' were co-written. The rest were Hugh's compositions. This is a very upbeat number featuring synthesised brass and is about the use and effects of cocaine. Apparently, 'uptown' is an expression originating from New York, meaning that you're taking cocaine. Hugh uses horse racing as an analogy to highlight the adrenaline rush of taking the drug, keeping such controversial matter hidden – remember 'Golden Brown'? The guitar intro sounds a bit like Eddie Cochran's 'C'mon Everybody', and it has a fast tempo that moves along nicely.

'Punch & Judy'

This features another lyric from Hugh inspired by an American girlfriend – a different one this time. There's a bit of 'hanky panky' hinted at between Judy and Punch when, once the audience have gone home following a show, 'she can lick him clean in style'. She also wants to go on holiday to 'lay back in the heat', but Punch (Hugh) wants to 'rest his aching feet'. However, they can't go on holiday just yet as 'there's a few more shows to pack in'. This alludes to the band's ever-busy touring schedule.

The brass is front and centre on this one, sounding, in parts, quite similar to Earth, Wind and Fire. The song, although generally considered by the band as a bit of a filler, became very popular live. It's one of those jaunty, jolly melodies underscored by a great rock 'n' roll bass line from JJ and ending with a saxophone solo that is the equal of any soul song. This song was the last song Hugh played with The Stranglers at Alexandra Palace on 11 August 1990.

'Spain'

Hugh loved travelling and went to Spain often as it was fairly easy and quick to get to. The first couple of verses are about the look and feel of Spain, but the last verse says that they have 'a lot of catching up to do' after the Franco regime and that they should 'take a lesson from their neighbours'. In other words, they should move forward into the future, unlike Portugal, which seemed to have stagnated. The female spoken part (by Candide) was taken from a documentary about General Franco and was originally spoken by his daughter Carmen. It was, therefore, fitting that she joined the Stranglers on stage in Spain to deliver the spoken word piece.

Dave's Hammond organ is well to the fore in this pop-rock track, with a superb solo just after the halfway point. Methinks that Hugh had been listening to some disco music before writing the music to some of these songs – especially this one. Also, Latham is all over this track, as it sounds just like a song Paul Young would sing.

'Laughing'

It seems fitting that on The Stranglers' most 'soulful' album, they should pay tribute to one of soul music's greatest singers, Marvin Gaye, who had been considered for production duties on the album and died during its recording. When Hugh brought the track to the band, it was an almost completed piece. Producer Latham recorded it with just Dave's keyboards and a drum machine, plus Hugh's vocal and the occasional piece of guitar. The title refers to the fact that Marvin Gaye had a very positive attitude to life and the line about 'lead poisoning' is a direct reference to Gaye's death after being shot by his own father. Hugh also lists some other ways in which he could have died, such as in a hotel bedroom or in a plane crash, rather than the tragic and untimely way he met his end. He also references Paul Young and his version of Gaye's 'Wherever I Lay My Hat'.

'Souls'

'Souls' is a song about Hugh's interest in Mayan culture after he read a book called *Incidents Of Travel In Yucatan*, written by John L. Stephens in 1843. He likens a woman to a god (or goddess), as he opines that a man raises a woman to deity status through his love. The Mayans were not averse to human sacrifice – usually by cutting out the heart of the victim – and this is also referenced. The 'steps' are the Mayan pyramids. Hugh seemed to have a keen interest in 'old' civilisations, and he would get all this out of his system on the next album. The backing vocals sound as if the recruited singers are taking part, but this isn't the case. It's all Hugh and JJ.

'Mad Hatter'

Inspired by a party full of eccentrics that Hugh went to, this track is a re-telling of those events through the lens of the Mad Hatter's tea party from *Alice In Wonderland* by Lewis Carroll, which has always been one of Hugh's favourite books. The friend who took him to the party is depicted as the Mad Hatter, and another person, who was always grinning, is portrayed as the Cheshire Cat. Regarded by Hugh as a throwaway track, it's a pleasant end to the vinyl album. And no, it's not a vibraphone – it's Dave on the keyboards. It trundles along very much like 'Old Codger'.

Other Contemporary Tracks

'Here And There'

Released as the B-side to 'Skin Deep', this was co-produced by the band and Laurie Latham. On the album, the band produced the tracks that originated in the first recording sessions and Latham the rest. This JJ lyric talks about missing someone (unspecified) but is also a paean to Europe as there are references to four countries. Also, JJ shows off some linguistic skills in the form of French ('Tu me manque'), Flemish ('Ik mis je') and Danish ('Savner dig'), all meaning 'I miss you'. He mentions Germany but doesn't include any German in the song. The backing singer is Dagmar Krause, who is known for her work with some of the avant-garde groups. It could almost be a Euro-disco song with its beat and 'happy' melody.

'In One Door'

Released as the flip to 'No Mercy', this was another co-produced with Latham. Hugh's lyric infers that he wasn't entirely happy with how things were in the band at that time, as he sings, 'Take me to another planet' and 'I can't abide all the fussing and fighting'. It could also relate to a relationship that was breaking down. To be honest, the members of the band had drifted slightly apart; they were all living separately from each other and had their own interests outside the band. They were only really coming together for meetings and work. It is interesting to note that although the band dealt with some downbeat subjects, the Euro-pop influence ensures a certain optimism in the music.

'Head On The Line'

Taken from the *No Mercy* EP, this is an anti-drug song from Mr Cornwell, who, by now, had come off all drugs. Hugh is asking people not to offer him drugs as he isn't interested in taking them. 'Head on the line' refers to him putting his head on the chopping block, with 'line' referring (in a subtle way) to drugs. Hugh had also come close to accidentally overdosing on cocaine, which is perhaps why he invokes others to 'make sure that your heart's beating on'. The song has an urgency about it, with semi-staccato melodies and a pounding beat. Hugh is not asking; he's demanding. It's almost punk-like in its sound.

'Achilles Heel'

This is a song that was recorded but was among those initially rejected for the album. It was done in a bit of a rush and sounds incomplete. If a bit more work had been done, it would have been a much better track and might have ended up on the album instead of being relegated to the B-side of 'Let Me Down Easy'. The words seemingly suggest that temptation is Hugh's 'Achilles heel' and he is trying to resist. The song builds up quite nicely, with the band sounding as though they are working well together. It has a slight feel of 'Hangin' Around'.

'Hot Club (Riot Mix)'

JJ and Dave came up with the music for this one and it was named after the Hot Club de Paris, which was a jazz group founded in France (surprise, surprise) in 1934 by guitarist Django Reinhardt and violinist Stephane Grappelli and lasted until 1948. They named it that because they likened the acoustic guitar and violin sounds (Dave on keyboards) they were making to the group's signature sound. Hugh suggested a bar atmosphere to underscore the track, so they added the sound effects of bottles, laughing, etc. It gives the song a superb, intimate atmosphere. And, of course, a fight breaks out. It's a great instrumental and was included as an extra track on the *No Mercy* EP.

'Place De Victoires'

This is a track from the 12" version of 'Let Me Down Easy'. In fact, it's an instrumental version of that song. The Place de Victoires is a circular plaza at the confluence of six streets, just behind The Louvre. In the centre stands a statue of King Louis XIV on a horse.

'Vladimir And The Beast'

The third instalment of the 'Vladimir' saga, with JJ on vocal duties. Hang on, I hear you ask, what happened to the second instalment? Well, 'Vladimir And Sergei' was a track included on *Fire And Water*, an album released in 1983 by JJ and Dave. 'Vladimir And The Beast' was issued on the 12" release of 'Skin Deep' and sees the band in the European style again. The whole song was put together by JJ and Dave and concerns Vladimir being sent to Afghanistan. There, whilst under the influence of hashish, he forms a 'close bond of affection' with Dimitri – a camel. He is then sent to East Germany (as it was then) to convalesce.

'Vladimir Goes To Havana'

The fourth episode in Vladimir's saga and released on the 12" limited edition of 'Let Me Down Easy'. Again, it was just Dave and JJ and it is a storyline not dissimilar to 'Vladimir And Olga'. Our hero manages to travel to Havana to continue his convalescence under Dr Buggerovski. We also learn Vlad's surname, which is Andropyournosin. Great names, boys! On a night out, he snorts what he thinks is sugar, but guess what? It's cocaine. The music is sped up and slowed down to give it a surreal touch. The song fades out with Vladimir's manic laughing.

Dreamtime (1986)

Personnel:
Hugh Cornwell: guitar, vocals.
Jean-Jacques Burnel: bass guitar, vocals
Dave Greenfield: keyboards, backing vocals
Jet Black: drums, percussion
Additional personnel:
Alex Gifford: saxophone
Hilary Kops: trumpet
Martin Veysey: trumpet
B.J. Cole: pedal steel guitar (on 'You'll Always Reap What You Sow')
Simon Morton: additional percussion
Recorded at ICP Studios, Brussels, Spaceward Studios, Cambridge, Crescent Studios, Bath, Farmyard Studios, Little Chalfont, between March and April 1986
Producer: The Stranglers and Mike Kemp
Engineer: Mike Kemp, Ted Hayton, Owen Morris
Original UK label and catalogue number: Epic Records EPC 26648
Released: 27 October 1986 (UK)
Highest chart position: UK: 16 (Silver), Australia: 64, Canada: 83, Netherlands: 60, New Zealand: 45, US: 172
Running time: 45.53
All tracks written by The Stranglers (Hugh Cornwell, Jean-Jacques Burnel, Dave Greenfield, Jet Black)

The gaps between albums were getting longer and there were almost two years before the next album. In the meantime, we'd had four singles: 'No Mercy', 'Let Me Down Easy', 'Nice In Nice' and 'Always The Sun', the latter two being preludes to the new album. Liberty had also released the album *Off The Beaten Track* (Liberty 5001), a collection of older, rare tracks which spent two weeks on the charts, reaching number 80. Added to that, we had a solo single from Hugh. 'One In A Million' was released in September 1985 on Portrait Records, a subsidiary of Epic (A6509). The drummer on the track was Pete Phipps, who had success the previous decade when he was in The Glitter Band.

By the time we got round to *Dreamtime,* Hugh and JJ were reconciled and were writing together again, But the band brought in Mike Kemp as the producer. Initially, the band had taken some songs to Laurie Latham because they wanted him to produce again, but he said that the songs needed more work and that the band should take a break. This is remembered differently by Latham and the band. Hugh and Latham say the songs weren't up to scratch. But JJ, Dave and Jet say they were unhappy with how the album was progressing and so sacked Latham. Either way, this soured the relationship between The Stranglers and Latham, as they needed someone who believed in them. Hugh would later work with the producer again on his 1997 solo album *Guilty*. Mike Kemp was known to JJ and Dave as he had produced their *Fire And Water* album in 1983. This change also led to a change of studios and they went into Spaceward Studios in Cambridge, where both JJ and Dave lived.

In keeping with the Aboriginal theme (there was even an Aboriginal script printed in the CD booklet), the cover shows four Aborigines in silhouette against the setting sun. This image was parodied by the official Stranglers fanzine *Strangled* by having, on the cover of Volume 2, number 26, an artist's impression of the album cover, with the four heads of the band members on the bodies of the silhouettes.

Of course, the band toured the album and they did it in two halves. The first half, in October and November 1986, saw The Stranglers perform their one and only sell-out headline show at Wembley Arena, and during the March 1987 jaunt, they sold out the Hammersmith Odeon three times!

Upon release, the album did moderately well, gaining yet another silver disc for the band. But even more importantly – or so it seemed at the time – *Dreamtime* charted in the US, reaching number 172, probably as a consequence 'Always The Sun's heavy airplay in 'the land of the free' and a tour the band undertook. The fact that the band had at last charted in America led some to believe that The Stranglers would go on to have more success in that territory. Sadly, that was not meant to be, as *Dreamtime* was the band's only album to make the US charts. In the UK, it reached number 16 during a six-week chart run. A pity, really, as it is quite a strong album.

'Always The Sun'

This is the A-side to the second single from the album, released on Epic Records (SOLAR 1) on 6 October 1986. It reached number 30 in the UK charts, spending five weeks worrying the chart compilers. The single charted in five other territories: Australia (number 21), France (number 15), Ireland (number 16), Poland (number seven) and the Netherlands (number 42). The non-album track 'Norman Normal' was on the B-side.

The single, remixed as 'Always The Sun (Sunny Side Up Mix)', was released on Christmas Eve 1990, with 'Burnham Beeches' on the flip side (Epic Records 6564307). Strangely, it did slightly better than the original, spending the same amount of time on the charts, but peaked one place higher at number 29. A 'Long Hot Sunny Side Up Mix' was issued on the 12" version of the re-release, with 'Burnham Beeches' and a live version of 'Straighten Out'. A CD single was also released, consisting of the 'Sunny Side Up Mix' and live versions of 'Nuclear Device', 'All Day And All Of The Night' and 'Punch And Judy'. By this time, Hugh had left the band, and although they kept his voice, they added extra guitar from new recruit John Ellis.

'Always The Sun' reversed the idea of people waking up when it's raining and wishing it was sunny: 'How many times have you woken up and prayed for the rain?'. It is also another of Hugh's songs where he berates people, inferring that the press, weathermen, politicians and even mothers always think they're right, but they are not necessarily so. The song is also about nuclear power (Hugh liked to get multiple meanings into his lyrics, as we have seen) and is even more poignant in the wake of the Chernobyl nuclear accident earlier in the year.

The chorus is great for a singalong, and the fans always give it their all when performed at gigs. The melody is gorgeous and is quite evocative. The guitar glissando seems – to me – a sound of summer and sunshine. The middle-eight has some great guitar work from Hugh, which is a live highlight (usually with Dave 'aahhhiing' in the background).

'Dreamtime'

This is the title track from the album, and a track, like 'Always The Sun', that was entirely written by Hugh. The song refers to the Aboriginal view of life, in which we don't own the world, but we are just passing through. 'I am there in the rock' enforces the Aboriginal theory that spirits of the dead are still with us, buried in everything around us. He also mentions the tradition of 'walkabout' in which the Aboriginal male, when they are aged between ten and 16, will live in the wilderness for up to six months alone, as a rite of passage.

Overall, a nice, medium-paced number with some fantastic, though understated, keyboard work from Dave and a good steady thudding beat courtesy of Jet's electronic drums.

'Was It You'

Written and sung by JJ, this is a return to his more aggressive self. Looking around the world and seeing hunger and poverty, political unrest, drugs, the AIDS crisis ('the genital disease') and everything else. He's pointing the finger and asking who is to blame.

A live version of the track was included on the B-side to 'Shakin' Like A Leaf', and it's the first song on the album to include brass. The band kept the brass in as it was part of the live set up and the brass parts freed up Dave to play more. It was meant to be released as the fifth single from the album, and a 7" version was edited but wasn't issued. In my ears, it has a slight 'Madness' sound, with the honking sax and the slight 'ska' vibe.

'You'll Always Reap What You Sow'

Another one written by JJ but sung by Hugh; JJ initially sang it using his 'operatic' voice, which Jet thought sounded awful. JJ was upset about that, but with help from producer Mike Kemp, Jet persuaded JJ to let Hugh sing it instead. Hugh was pleased to do it and said in 2001 that it was 'a heartfelt lyric and was one of the best songs he [JJ] ever wrote'.

At JJ's suggestion, they brought in Brian John 'B.J.' Cole to play pedal steel guitar, which Hugh couldn't play. To list B.J.'s recording C.V. would take all day, but some of the artists he has worked for include Elton John, The Moody Blues, Humble Pie, Uriah Heep, Katie Melua and Sting.

The lyrics could be about Hugh and JJ's fractured relationship with him, as hinted at in the words, 'Don't forget I loved you once'. And 'To think I knew you when you had nothing at all'.

A slower number, the bass drum provides the pulse whilst the guitar plays big, strummed, open chords with a delay effect, which gives the song a dreamy airiness. The pedal steel guitar adds an ethereal quality to the music.

'Ghost Train'

This Hugh song, from a bass riff by JJ, is about each band member's desire to take control; Hugh likens it to trying to drive a train. As the four of them were all different characters, they were pulling in different directions: 'Who's qualified to drive the ghost train'. There is also a little reference to the possibility of band members still using drugs: 'The driver is blind when there's snow on the line'. 'Snowblind' is a word used to describe someone who is 'out of it' and incapable. Hugh speaks the track, as he couldn't come up with a suitable melody for the vocal line. Jet's drum machine gives us the train going down the tracks, and it sounds like the train whistle is a mixture of guitar and keyboard.

'Nice In Nice'

The first single taken from the album, this was released on Epic (EPC 650055) in August 1986 with 'Since You Went Away' on the B-side. The 12" version had the live recordings of 'Midnight Summer Dream' and 'The European Female', recorded at Le Zenith in Paris on 29 April 1985. The single spent five weeks in the UK charts, peaking at number 30, whilst abroad, it only reached number 19 in Ireland.

Written by JJ, the track is surprisingly NOT about the problems they had in Nice back in 1980. It's about his wife. But even though he says that she has a lovely smile, she seems to be spoilt: 'She's got diamond rings from her dad' and 'She owns the ground she walks on and she walks all over you'. Typical JJ twist in the tail there. Strangely, since this was not about their experiences in Nice, the single had a picture of the band in custody on the front and the video had the band in prison uniforms.

This song rattles along at a good pace, with JJ giving some breathy vocals. The drums, sadly, are obviously electronic.

'Big In America'

The third single from the album, this was released in December 1986 on Epic Records (HUGE 1). Although it spent six weeks on the UK charts, it fared disappointingly, reaching only number 48. The B-side was a non-album track called 'Dry Day'. The single also reached number 28 in Ireland, number 50 in Germany and number 38 in Belgium.

Hugh wrote this song, listing some of his observations about America. For instance, the title refers to the fact that everything appears huge in America, including people: 'She wore the pants 'cross a big expanse'. A news story that cockroaches had been found in television sets on the 25th floor of some buildings led to the reference to a cockroach in the first line. Also, the line, 'And when you're big in America/You like to live in America', is self-explanatory, but The Stranglers never really made it big in the US and so had no desire to live there.

Another seemingly brass-laden song, the only brass instrument used is a saxophone (which is really a woodwind instrument). The other brass is courtesy of Dave's synthesiser.

'Shakin' Like A Leaf"

This is a reworked version of a song originally recorded for *Aural Sculpture* but rejected by the record company. The original version was issued as the fourth single in February 1987 on Epic Records (SHEIK 1), with 'Hitman' on the flip side. The single spent four weeks on the UK charts, reaching the dizzying heights of number 58, the lowest-charting single so far. The record company were desperate to get something out of the album, which is why they opted to release a fourth single, something never done by the band before. Obviously, it didn't work and the single failed to chart anywhere else.

The band liked the song, which Hugh had demoed at home, but it was changed into a 'swing'-type number at the instigation of JJ. For the count-in, Hugh's voice was put through a 'harmoniser' to make it lower in pitch.

Lyrically, the song is about the uncertainty of life and how it can change in a flash. 'Lying in your bed/wide awake with sleepy head' suggests that the subject of the song is being kept awake with worry.

'Mayan Skies'

JJ and Hugh wrote 'Mayan Sies', with Hugh writing the melody and lyrics and JJ the bass line. Some excellent keyboard work from Dave gives the song an atmospheric 'wash'. This was inspired by Hugh's Mexican sojourns and the music and lyrics combine perfectly to conjure up a picture of the land. There's even some playful trumpet reminiscent of Herb Alpert and the Tijuana Brass. The colours red, green and yellow refer to the colours of the Mexican flag (there is only a little bit of yellow, I concede, but it's important). Red signifies blood; green is the jungle and yellow is the sun, although Hugh also uses it to signify the gold that the Spanish invaders looted when they conquered the country between 1519 and 1521.

'Too Precious'

JJ and Hugh also wrote this, with superb contributions from both Dave and Jet. Another descriptive musical vista, this time South Africa is the subject rather than South America, although there is a Latin-tinged vibe. The 'few who had plenty' line points the finger at the minority in South Africa who held most of the money (in other words, the whites). The 'poor who were rich' means that although the majority of blacks were financially poor, they were rich in heritage, and the 'rocks that were shining' are the diamonds that are at the heart of the South African economy. There was a lot of controversy about the segregation in South Africa and the Apartheid system, and many artists refused to perform there until the restrictions were lifted. The Stranglers were, in fact, offered a gig in the entertainment centre of Sun City but declined to go.

I have to say that, in my opinion, it's a rather lacklustre end to the original vinyl album. Perhaps a 'punchier' song should have been used to make it more memorable.

Other Contemporary Tracks

'Since You Went Away'

The B-side to 'Nice In Nice'. Not one of The Stranglers' more polished pieces. Dave is very busy on the keyboards and no doubt wishes he had a few more arms. It's a JJ song, with Mr Burnel apparently lamenting the loss of a girlfriend. With a bit more work, this would have made a nice addition to the album, and there is a hint of 'European Female' in the music.

'Norman Normal'

'Norman Normal' was an outtake from *Aural Sculpture* and the B-side to 'Aways The Sun' and was produced by Laurie Latham. It's a quirky one from JJ that leans towards psychedelia in the manner of early Pink Floyd when Syd Barratt was still with them. The lyrics are a bit wacky, too. Norman is the epitome of bland. He had his wife, kids and pets. But then he changes. Is he a criminal with his friends already living on the Costa Del Crime? Or is he a sailor, serving King and Country, with a tendency to dress up in women's clothing to become 'ginger beer' ('queer' – 'homosexual') on a Saturday night? You get the drift. Subject-wise, it's in the same vein as the protagonist in The Kinks' *Soap Opera* by Ray Davies (1975), in which the 'hero' – also called Norman – imagines that he is a pop star, pretending to be 'normal' for research into songs.

'Dry Day'

The B-side to 'Shakin' Like A Leaf'. Hugh, in 2001, said that this was overdone and the drum machine makes it sound like The Human League. Seemingly, it refers to bullying: 'Just let them talk/about your walk' and 'Could you/ Turn the other cheek?' The chorus – 'Will it be a dry day?/Or will there be a tear there in your eye?' – makes clear the potential distress caused by such behaviour, but 'dry day' suggests that the protagonist feels the need to bottle up their feelings. A great saxophone and keyboard-led intro sets the scene for the rest of the song.

'Hit Man'

The B-side to 'Shakin' Like A Leaf' was originally recorded for *Aural Sculpture* but ultimately rejected for that album. Hugh wrote this one but is extremely unhappy with the finished product. He feels that it should have been re-recorded. His lyrics liken a photographer to a hitman (professional assassin), as they are always taking shots at people. Jet is playing with the drum machine and seemingly trying every setting (with a drum riff a bit like 'Mama' by Genesis), and Dave valiantly plays some good keyboards with different soundscapes not unlike 1980s hitmakers Heaven 17. When EMI decided to release a career-spanning (1977-1991) double CD in 1997, this track provided the inspiration for the name – *The Hit Men*.

'Burnham Beeches'

This is an instrumental originally intended to be the B-side of 'Was It You?' but was shelved when the single wasn't released. It leaked out on the re-release of 'Always The Sun' in 1990. The band's production manager Sil Willcox added some guitar – he later became the band's manager (after auditioning to become the band's new singer). Although pleasant enough and keyboard-dominated, it's little more than filler.

'Midnight Summer Dream/European Female (Live)'

The B-side to 'Nice In Nice', recorded at Le Zenith in Paris on 29 April 1985.

Above: The Stranglers 1975 – 1990. Top: Hugh, Jet. Bottom: Dave, JJ. (*Alamy*)

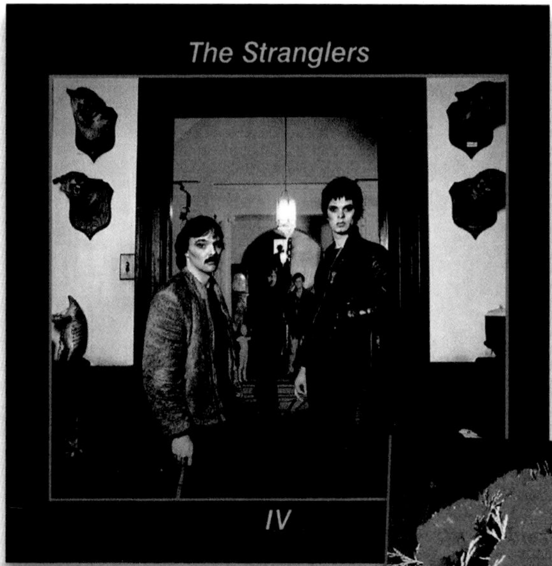

Left: The album that started it all. *Rattus Norvegicus*. (*United Artists Records*)

Right: The chocolate box wreath on *No More Heroes*. (*United Artists Records*)

Left: Off we go with the 'obvious' covers, *Black And White*. (*United Artists Records*)

Right: A limited edition 3D cover for *The Raven*. Guess what's on the cover. (*United Artists Records*)

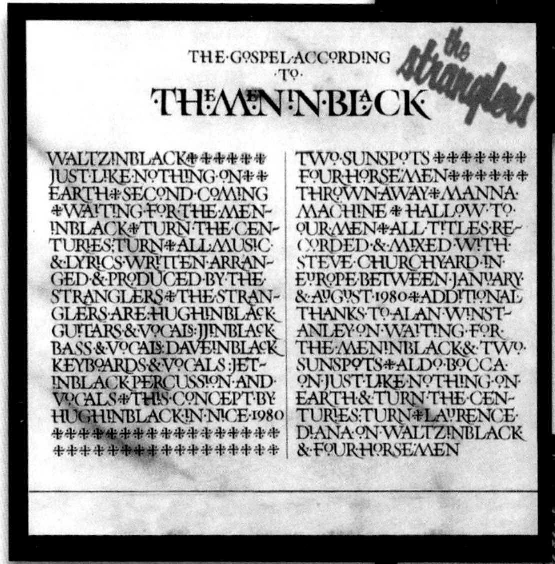

Left: A Biblical script for *The Gospel According To The Meninblack*. (*Liberty Records*)

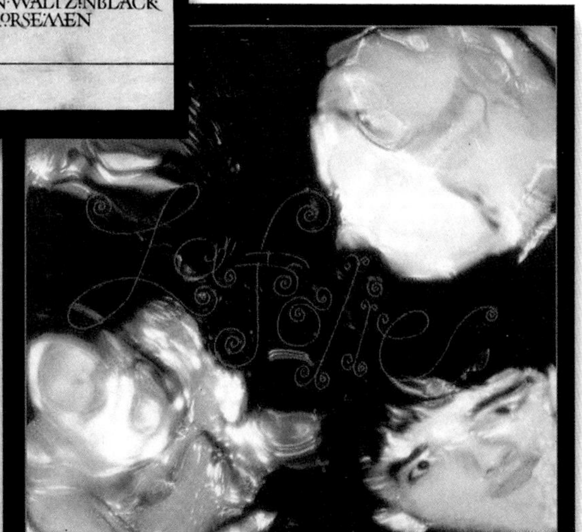

Right: The psychedelic cover to *La Folie*. At least the band were featured. (*Liberty Records*)

Left: Performing 'No More Heroes' on Dutch TV show *TopPop*.

Right: Still on *TopPop*. What has Hugh seen? And a hungry JJ about to eat the microphone.

Left: The Lounge Lizards performing 'Golden Brown' in its promotional video.

Right: Dave and Jet ham it up in the video for 'Golden Brown'.

Left: Jet working hard in the video for 'Skin Deep'.

Right: Dave in the video for 'Skin Deep'.

Left: A sinister cover for *Feline*. The black panther sums up the band. (*Epic Records*)

Right: The *Aural Sculpture* cover, taken in Trafalgar Square. (*Epic Records*)

Left: The Aboriginal inspired cover for *Dreamtime*. (*Epic Records*)

Right: *10*. Hugh's last album, with The Stranglers looking like the world's leaders. (*Epic Records*)

Left: Enter Paul Roberts and John Ellis. The original UK cover for *Stranglers In The Night*. North America's cover was white instead of dark grey. (*Psycho Records*)

Right: The frayed rope cover of *About Time*. Were The Stranglers about to snap? (*Castle Communications*)

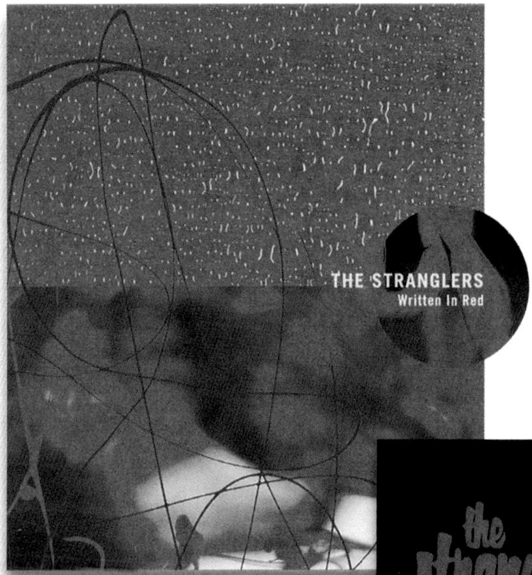

Left: The 13th studio album. Unlucky for some, but not as far as the author is concerned. The *Written In Red* album contains one of my favourite Stranglers tracks – 'Summer In The City'. (*Castle Communications*)

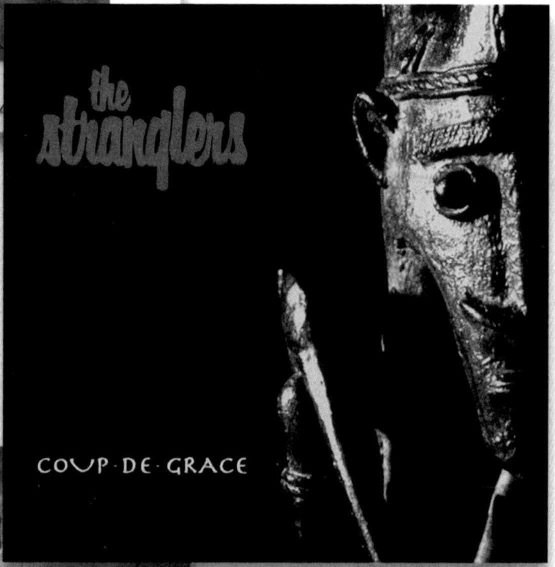

Right: JJ reasserted his leadership of The Stranglers with *Coup De Grace*. (*Eagle Records*)

Left: Goodbye to John and hello to Baz Warne. Back to EMI for the sublime *Norfolk Coast*. (*EMI Records*)

Right: Back to being a quartet following the departure of Paul Roberts. *Suite XIV* carried on The Stranglers' resurgence. (*Liberty Records / EMI*)

Left: The final album with Jet Black. The rather disturbing cover of *Giants*. (*Coursegood / Absolute*)

Right: The latest album so far. The thoughtful *Dark Matters*. Dave Greenfield's last album. (*Coursegood / Absolute*)

Above: The Stranglers 2000 – 2006. From left: JJ, Dave, Paul, Jet, Baz Warne. (*Cruisin' Music*)

Right: Paul Roberts playing bass on 'Don't Bring Harry'. (*Paul Roberts Collection*)

Above: JJ, Dave and Baz at The Roundhouse. 4 November 2007. (*Steve Woof*)

Below: Jet at The Roundhouse. 4 November 2007. (*Steve Woof*)

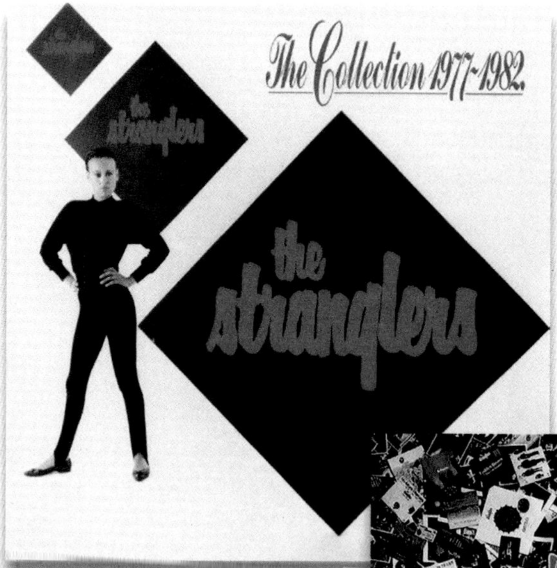

Left: Probably the worst Stranglers cover. *The Collection 1977-82*. (*Liberty Records*)

Right: A better hits collection, *Greatest Hits 1977-90*, the band's only platinum disc. (*Liberty Records*)

Left: The compilation that never was. The *4240* album cover. (*Sony/BMG*)

Right: On to the live albums and the 'handy' *Live (X Cert)* album. (*United Artists Records*)

Left: *All Live And All Of The Night* was named after the hit single of the same name, which wasn't actually on the original vinyl album. (*Epic Records*)

Right: The cover of the Dave Greenfield tribute album, given away with pre-orders of *Dark Matters*. (*Coursegood*)

Left: The Stranglers 2006 – 2018. From left: Baz, Jet, JJ, Dave. (*Coursegood*)

Right: The Stranglers 2018 – 2020. From left: Dave, Jim Macaulay, Baz, JJ. (*David Boni*)

Left: JJ and Baz in full flow. (*Hiroki Nishioki*)

Right: The Stranglers' current writing team. JJ and Baz.

Left: The Stranglers 2020 – present. From left, Jim, Baz, JJ, Toby Hounsham. (*Cruisin' Music*)

Right: JJ Burnel and the author at Manchester Academy, 3 November 2007. (*Martin Hutchinson*)

Left: A signed copy of the 2008 *FortyTwoForty* tour brochure. (*Martin Hutchinson*)

10 (1990)

Personnel:
Hugh Cornwell: guitar, lead and backing vocals.
Jean-Jacques Burnel: bass guitar, lead and backing vocals
Dave Greenfield: keyboards, backing vocals
Jet Black: drums, percussion
Additional personnel:
Alex Gifford: saxophone
Sid Gauld: trumpet
Chris Lawrence: trombone
Stuart Brooks: trumpet solo (on 'Sweet Smell Of Success')
Simon Morton: congas (on 'Sweet Smell Of Success')
Tere Baker: voice (on 'Let's Celebrate')
Pamela G: voice (on 'Where I Live')
Recorded at Wisseloord Studios, Hilversum, Netherlands, in Autumn 1989
Producer: Roy Thomas Baker
Engineer: Timm Baldwin
Original UK label and catalogue number: Epic Records 4664831
Released: March 1990 (UK)
Highest chart position: UK: 15 (Silver), Netherlands: 71
Running time: 36.23
All tracks written by The Stranglers (Hugh Cornwell, Jean-Jacques Burnel, Dave Greenfield, Jet Black) except '96 Tears' by Rudy Martinez

There was yet another lengthy wait – three and a half years in fact – before we had *10*, Hugh's last album and the last to feature brass. The gap between albums was due to the band's extensive touring throughout the rest of 1987. They then spent the whole of 1988 recording tracks at their own studio that Jet built (in just two weeks) in JJ's garden in Cambridgeshire. The band took the recorded songs to the record company and A&R head Muff Winwood said that the songs needed better production. He brought in Roy Thomas Baker, who had worked with the likes of Queen and Pilot because – as Hugh put it in 2001 – 'he could produce the sound that the Americans wanted'. The band were of the opinion that the way forward was America, thanks to the last album making the American charts.

The band were also on a bit of a high after a top ten single in the UK with a cover of The Kinks' 'All Day And All Of The Night'. Hugh, however, was the anomaly as he was miffed that the band were having success with other people's material and the success of the live album *All Live And All Of The Night,* which became a Gold record for the band. He wanted more success with brand new, band-written material rather than end up paying royalties to other songwriters. EMI also released a remixed version of 'Grip' entitled 'Grip '89' (as was the vogue at the time, releasing remixed tracks), with 'Waltzinblack' on the B-side, which was being used as the theme to Keith

Floyd's TV programme at the time. This was to tie in with the *Singles (The UA Years)* compilation album, which charted (See 'Assorted Compilation Albums'). Furthermore, Hugh released another solo album entitled *Wolf*, his first after signing a deal with Virgin Records, from which the single 'Another Kind Of Love' was taken. Moreover, JJ released a solo album on Epic entitled *Un Jour Parfait*.

When touring the album, the band brought in John Ellis as a second guitarist to fill out the sound and to give Hugh a bit more freedom to sing without having to worry about playing the guitar at the same time. Little did he know what would happen next. Jet Black had his first outing of bad health – the deadly shingles – during a tour of the United States in 1987. Hugh's mate Robert Williams, the drummer with Captain Beefheart – and Hugh's collaborator on *Nosferatu* – stood, or rather sat, in for him.

10 is generally regarded as the least successful album; it was at least a return to a conventional rock sound after the 'softer' albums. Despite this, it was still good enough to make the top 20 albums, reaching number 15 (and another silver disc for the collection) but spending only four weeks on the listings – their shortest so far.

The album cover is very interesting, with the band poking fun at the world's leaders. The album is called *10*: it's the tenth studio album the band had recorded; there were ten tracks on the original album ... so guess how many world leaders are depicted on the album's cover? Yes, you've guessed it. From left to right, we have Yasser Arafat (Jet), Rajiv Gandhi (Dave), Pope John Paul II (JJ), Mikhail Gorbachev (Dave), Margaret Thatcher (JJ), George (no Dubya) Bush (Hugh), Fidel Castro (Jet), Colonel Gadaffi (Hugh), Benazir Bhutto (JJ) and Joshua Nkomo (Jet). The portrayals of Jet as Arafat and Nkomo are notable; he appears to be staring at himself and the smile on Arafat's face is just about the closest you'll get to a picture of Jet smiling! And we have JJ in drag – twice! (and not for the first time either, as both JJ and Dave had dressed in drag to promote their *Fire And Water* album).

With the benefit of hindsight, we all know what was going to happen just five months after the release of the album, but the collective impression of the album gives an indication of Hugh's alienation from the band. All the band regard *10* as their worst album, but Hugh thinks it was their best.

'Sweet Smell Of Success'

This was the second single from the album, released in April 1990 on Epic Records (TEARS 2) with 'Motorbike' and 'Something' on the flip. Sadly, it wasn't – as the title might suggest – a success, spending only two weeks on the UK charts and only reaching number 65. It failed to chart anywhere else.

It was written by Hugh and JJ, with a lot of input from Dave. The lyrics, by Hugh, speak of the band's current state from his standpoint. They had tasted success, but they wanted more. 'You think you'll win next time you play' alludes to the band's misguided hope for the next single to be a hit, especially as Hugh thought that the songs on *10* were particularly good.

A terrific and pacey intro sets the scene for a very commercial-sounding track, with keyboard and trumpet solos in the middle.

'Someone Like You'

Another song by Hugh, this one showcasing a fairground-like Farfisa organ sound (also used extensively by Mike Oldfield in his early work), courtesy of Dave, who had a lot of input into the whole album.

The lyrics are about Hugh's new girlfriend, who made a big impression on him, hence the analogy of an earthquake; in fact, there are a few references to weather in the song. Hugh was a great admirer of The Kinks' Ray Davies and the fact that he liked to put humour into his words. Hugh employs a similar tactic with lines like, 'My roof was raised as I was snoring so comfortably', hinting at the sudden chaos that the girl caused in his life. The fact that there is no gap between 'Sweet Smell Of Success' and this hints at a similarity in the songs. Both are powerful and have a similar beat.

'96 Tears' (Rudy Martinez)

A return to the Farfisa organ sound for this cover of the 1966 hit by ? and The Mysterians. The writer, Rudy Martinez, is ? (or Question Mark). And no, The Mysterians does not refer to *Captain Scarlet And The Mysterons*, but a 1957 Japanese film called *The Mysterians*.

This was the first single taken from the album, released by Epic in February 1990 (TEARS 1), and reached number 17 in the UK charts in a six-week chart run. It included 'Instead Of This' on the B-side (as well as 'Poisonality' on the 12" version). It was a decent hit in Ireland, reaching number nine.

The song itself is about the break-up of a relationship and was suggested to the band by producer Roy Thomas Baker.

Following the failure of 'Sweet Smell Of Success', it meant that of the last five singles released by the band, the only hits had been cover versions – '96 Tears' and 'All Day And All Of The Night' – which frustrated the band, as they regarded themselves as songwriters as well as performers, especially Hugh.

'In This Place'

This bleak song came from JJ, and again, he uses his 'operatic' voice. Very similar to The Beach Boys' 'In My Room', it explores loneliness. It could also allude to the fact that Hugh and JJ weren't getting along like they used to, hence the lyric: 'And the ghosts we thought we'd carefully laid to rest ... Carefully laid to rest have returned'. The pair had argued in the past, but things came to a head again during the making of *10*; JJ was unhappy with Hugh's work ethic and he thought that Hugh wasn't committed to the album. Yes, it's a bit bleak, but there are some great choral harmonies.

'Let's Celebrate'

An upbeat song from Hugh and one with lots of brass – presumably to appeal to American listeners. The lyrics refer to the multiple ways of celebrating something, although there could be an allusion to sex: 'Let me get to taste your honey child'. The spoken bit is by Baker's wife Tere, and the use of 'backward' sounding music is inspired – it gives the song a psychedelic vibe.

'Man Of The Earth'

Slated to be the third single but pulled after the failure of 'Sweet Smell Of Success'. Hugh is in Ray Davies mode again and Jet Black thought it could have been a hit. Although sounding quite upbeat, the lyric is rather sad, with Hugh putting himself into the shoes of an office worker and having to plan things months ahead: 'The city blues they strike again'. The 'man of the earth' wants to escape to the country, which was also in Hugh's mind at the time, as he explained in 2001 in the *Song By Song* book. There's more bass on this one, as producer Baker asked JJ to come back in and re-record some of the bass parts. This led to a souring of the relationship between the bassist and producer.

'Too Many Teardrops'

Hugh is commenting about his position in the band on this song. The original producer Owen Morris thought this was a very commercial track when first recorded at JJ's home studio, but both JJ and Dave thought that Hugh was dominating the album, which disillusioned him. The song is about crying and its therapeutic value. The intro is the nearest this album gets to sounding like The Stranglers of old, with the bass having a harder edge and Dave's keyboards coming to the fore.

'Where I Live'

The contract with Baker seems to have been for him to produce just ten tracks for the album; after all, the album was called *10* and it was The Stranglers' tenth studio album. Hugh said in 2001 that this track was included and 'Instead Of This' was dropped, but both should have appeared on the finished album.

JJ wrote and sang the lyrics, which are about the area of Cambridgeshire where he was living at the time. He mentions the pub, playing cricket and his motorcycle. He also namechecks himself and his wife. Furthermore, he nods back to his rock star life and getting girls into trouble: 'Who is the man with the double-barrelled gun?/(My Daddy)'. For a change, JJ is singing this one like a 'normal' rock singer and not snarling his way through the lyrics.

'Out Of My Mind'

The Stranglers tap into their 'psychedelic' side again here with a multi-tracked vocal in the intro from Hugh describing an out-of-body experience, backed by some backward echo and later some backward guitar. Hugh says that the song has a double meaning: firstly, it's about tripping ('your smell works better than glue') and also about a woman you can't get out of your mind ('But when you smile, my day gets brighter'). At the end of the song, there is no break between tracks, and it goes straight into the final song on the album.

'Never To Look Back'

A JJ song to close the album and one displaying a haunting sound. JJ was beginning to see things differently – perhaps maturing. He sings, 'It's not that easy/Never to look back' because 'The years distort the lies/We take for fact'. He also mentions that although he wore a black shirt, he wasn't one; that is, he didn't have extreme political views.

A very good title and one the band used when they did, in fact, look back. When the band released the DVD *The Video Collection 1983 – 2012* in 2013, they called the collection *Never To Look Back*. It's a great closing track with the lead vocal from JJ being exceptional.

Other Contemporary Tracks

'Instead Of This'

The B-side of '96 Tears' and one of Hugh's favourite songs by JJ, even though he thinks it's about him. It certainly appears so, with lyrics like 'I don't want to see you anymore' and 'I just want to see you walk out that door'. However, JJ told this author in 2023 that the song isn't about Hugh, so it could be about an ex-partner.

It was recorded in the first batch of recordings for the album and, therefore, produced by the band with Owen Morris. There's some excellent guitar from Hugh on this one, sounding not unlike Carlos Santana in places.

'Poisonality'

This was the B-side, along with 'Instead Of This', of the 12" version of '96 Tears'. Another song that came from the first batch of recordings, this was written by Hugh and showcases a great melody. To be honest, the mix isn't great and the vocals are a bit fuzzy, but Hugh makes up for it with his emulations of a slide guitar.

'Motorbike'

Produced by the band with Owen Morris, this was the B-side to 'Sweet Smell Of Success', a song by JJ about his obsession with motorbikes. Always intended to be a B-side, it shows that JJ was capable of a bit of wordplay, too. When he asks, 'Do you wanna ride my motorbike?', is it really his bike he is letting them ride? JJ's 'breathy' vocals add a touch of 'sexiness' to the track.

'Something'

This was the B-side to the 12" version of 'Sweet Smell Of Success', another JJ song from the first batch of tracks. A slightly dodgy vocal from him, but overall, this is a great and heartfelt song about his son. With a bit more work, this slower song could have made the album.

'You'

This was the B-side to the re-issue of 'Golden Brown' in 1991 on Epic Records (6567617) and is a song about a girl he was obsessed with. A lot of work went into this track, which was produced by Laurie Latham and written by Hugh in 1984. In the end, despite all the work over three months, it didn't seem to be going anywhere, so it was discarded. It's a bit funky, though, with an insistent beat and staccato guitar. The bass and drums are quite low in the mix. Perhaps they should have gone back to this track and done some more work on it.

'Viva Vlad!'

The fifth instalment of the 'Vlad' saga became the B-side to 'All Day And All Of The Night'. In this episode, Vladimir is arrested and set adrift in a dinghy. Despite shooting at him, he escaped intact and fell asleep, waking up when the boat ran ashore and finding himself in Mexico. He settled into his new life there, but a map showed him how close he was to Miami and he started planning his next adventure. The music was used by British TV chef Keith Floyd for his TV show.

'All Day And All Of The Night' (Ray Davies)

A studio version of the track that gave the band a top ten hit in the UK. It spent seven weeks in the UK charts, reaching number seven (see 'Live Albums'). The Stranglers' version is very faithful to The Kinks' original.

Stranglers In The Night (1992)

Personnel:
Paul Roberts: vocals
Jean-Jacques Burnel: bass guitar, vocals
John Ellis: guitar, vocals
Dave Greenfield: keyboards, vocals
Jet Black: drums, percussion
Additional personnel:
Simon Morton: additional percussion
Recorded at Steptoe Recorders, Studio Audio, Dojo, Jacobs Studios, Sarm East, Sarm West, Metropolis, between 1991 and 1992
Producer: Mike Kemp
Engineer: Richard Norris
Original UK label and catalogue number: Psycho Records WOLCD 1030
Released: September 1992 (UK)
Highest chart position: UK: 33
Running time: 51.28
All tracks written by The Stranglers (Paul Roberts, Jean-Jacques Burnel, John Ellis, Dave Greenfield, Jet Black)

Following the release of *10*, the band were rocked by Hugh's sudden departure, although it wasn't totally unexpected as he had been moving further and further away from The Stranglers and was becoming more disillusioned. The band played the last gig of a tour at London's Alexandra Palace on 11 August 1990, and unbeknownst to anybody except himself, Hugh had decided that afternoon that this would be his last gig with the band. In fact, the only person aware of his imminent departure was second guitarist John Ellis, when, after the show, Hugh said, 'Have a nice life' and left. Deciding not to participate in the after-show party, he went out with friends. The next day, he rang his now-former bandmates to break the news. Jet was first and wasn't surprised; then Dave, who was totally shocked. The last and most difficult call was to JJ. Both he and Hugh remember this conversation being emotional. It left a bitter taste in everyone's mouth that, to some extent, still lingers today. Both Hugh and JJ previously said that if anyone left the band, it would be the end for The Stranglers, but the next time the pair met up – at a meeting in the band's accountants' office a couple of months later – it was apparent that JJ, Dave and Jet decided to carry on. In fact, the only people who weren't sad that Hugh left were those at Epic, who, thanks to a clause in the band's recording contract, could now be dropped by the label, which they duly did. However, they were still commercially savvy enough to release a compilation album – *Greatest Hits 1977-90* – featuring tracks from their time with Epic and also EMI. It reached number nine in the UK charts and a single released at the time, 'Always The Sun (Sunny Side Up Mix)', reached number 29, one place higher than its original release.

The hunt was now on to find a replacement for Hugh; in terms of a guitarist, they didn't have to look far. John Ellis played with the band as second guitarist and had deputised for Hugh at the Rainbow gig when Hugh was in jail. John William Ellis was born in Kentish Town, London, on 1 June 1952. He co-founded the band Bazooka Joe in 1970 and The Vibrators in 1976 but left in 1978. He toured and recorded with Peter Gabriel and Peter Hammill. As well as playing guitar on the *10* tour, he had previous experience with The Stranglers. The very first Vibrators gig was supporting The Stranglers at Page Green School, and according to John, the audience consisted of 'three people and a dog'. He then worked with JJ as part of his Euroman band when JJ toured his solo *Euroman Cometh* album, and just prior to the *10* tour, he played and recorded with JJ and Dave in their Purple Helmets side project (see 'Solo Work').

John told me:

> When I was asked to join full-time, I was working with Peter Hammill, but with him, there was no songwriting potential for me. I joined for the songwriting mainly. They had been a brilliant band, but sadly, Hugh's departure had knocked the stuffing out of them. Anyway, I was happy to be in a waged scenario.

The band and management still had to find a singer. They auditioned just four contenders. Boo Hewerdine from the rock band The Bible, Ian McNabb from The Icicle Works, an unknown singer called Paul Roberts and The Stranglers' own production manager Sil Willcox, who would later become their manager – and still is today. He told me in 2023 that 'I put my hat in the ring for Hugh's job, but the band's producer and their management at the time had a soft spot for Paul. I think I was a bit sad at the time, but I probably didn't think I would get it anyway'. In fact, Sil was second in the race. He would later take over as manager (with Trevor Long).

Paul Roberts was chosen to be the new singer. He was born in Chiswick, London, on 31 December 1959 and played in a few self-formed bands until meeting Colin Johnson, with a view to getting his current band signed up. Colin, at the time, was part of The Stranglers' team and suggested that Paul audition as singer. This was a surprise to Paul because, even though he was a fan of the band, he had no idea that Hugh had left. His appointment was confirmed in November 1990 and announced the following January. The band then had to rehearse three dozen songs for a tour, which started at the Rodon Club in Athens, Greece, on 22 February 1991. Two of the songs in the set were new ones that would appear on the next album: 'Wet Afternoon' and a ballad, 'Heaven Or Hell', both written by John Ellis.

In Paul Roberts, the band now had a showman rather than a frontman, as Hugh was inclined not to be too mobile. Paul strutted around the stage like Mick Jagger and, famously, at the 'Friday The Thirteenth' gig, dived off the stage into the audience!

To the fans, it seemed like business as usual, but according to John, the rest of the original band were in turmoil. 'It looked like to me that JJ wasn't interested much in writing stuff and it seemed that only Jet was enthusiastic'. The main problem for the band now was that the record label had dropped them, so they had no outlet for new material. This was solved by the band investing heavily in their own record label – Psycho (named by JJ perhaps), a subsidiary of China Records. Most of the music for the band's first post-Hugh album had already been put together by JJ and John, and indeed, Paul had been given a cassette of some of the music to put lyrics to.

Six months before the new album came out, EMI released a live album – *Live At The Hope And Anchor*, a recording of a full gig from 1977. Furthermore, Epic released *All Twelve Inches*, an album of a dozen remixed tracks. It didn't chart.

The 11th studio album, known as *Stranglers In The Night*, or just *In The Night*, was recorded throughout 1991 and 1992 in a number of studios and was released in the autumn of 1992. Depending on where you lived, you had a choice of colours. Both versions had the band logo without the 'the' and the album title, with a 'spooky' face and a rat where the mouth should be. In the UK, the face was black on a dark grey background, whereas the North American version's background was white and contained three extra tracks, which were used as B-sides. In August, the first single off the album was released in a number of formats – 'Heaven Or Hell', with 'Disappear', 'Coffee Shop', 'Hanging Around (live)', 'Vicious Circles' and 'Brainbox' as extra tracks scattered across the various formats.

The album only graced the charts for one week at number 33, which was rather disappointing for the whole band, especially as it was a far better album than *10*, with a returning Mike Kemp producing an album that had a harder edge.

'Time To Die'

This is mainly instrumental, with the lyrics inspired by the film *Blade Runner* and the science fiction writer Iain M Banks. A great Shadows-inspired guitar riff and swirling synthesisers adorn this track. According to John Ellis, everyone contributed to this, although JJ apparently came up with the tune, which sounds similar to Monty Norman's 'James Bond Theme'. Strangely, although this is a great song live, it only appears on one official live album – *Themeninblackintokyo*.

The superb guitar riff at the start of the song introduces us to John Ellis and makes the whole thing sound like a film or television theme. Paul Roberts wrote the spoken word section at the beginning and JJ came up with the title.

For the first time, all the lead vocals on a Stranglers album are by the same person – Paul. The vocals here are rather depressing as Paul seems to be referring to life experiences that have left an impression – 'Neon storms' brings to mind a world where the skies are full of pollution and artificial lights. He also mentions hope, but it will all disappear and so it's 'Time to die'.

'Sugar Bullets'

The second single taken from the album, released in October 1992 on Psycho Records (PSYCD 002). The B-side was 'So Uncool' and an extended version of 'Sugar Bullets'.

This rocker features words and music from John. The term 'Sugar Bullets' is a term used by a political organisation to denote something that seems benign but is, in fact, malignant, particularly in reference to the tension between the US and China at the time, hence the use of 'Chairman' and 'the red man'. John is asking the government to use 'sugar bullets'; instead of using money to fund a war, using it for food aid to that country.

This fast-paced number was rush-released to cash in on the fact that Simon Bates started playing it on Radio One. Sadly, this was the first physically released single by the band not to enter the charts anywhere and they only did it once more. It is a shame that it didn't do well, as it is a more traditional Stranglers-type song.

'Heaven Or Hell'

Released on 10 August 1992 on Psycho Records (WOXCD 2025), this heralded the album, which was released a month later. It reached number 46 in the UK charts, spending two weeks there, and got to number 77 in The Netherlands. 'Disappear', 'Coffee Shop', 'Hanging Around (live)', 'Vicious Circles' and 'Brainbox' were extra tracks scattered across the various formats, which were available as a 12", double CD and cassette.

Another of John Ellis' songs, he tells me that it is a philosophical look at life. You can't tell if you're in Heaven or Hell. He said of its poor chart performance: 'it was a disaster to release a ballad and not a rocker as the first single'. But it must be said that the guitar work is of the highest order, especially the delicate intro and the solo towards the end.

Paul's vocals on this, and indeed many songs, sound very much like Hugh, which was one of the reasons he was picked for the job. He had a talent for being able to sing in 'different' voices; he could be 'Hugh' or others. This proved useful when recording, as he could change his voice to suit the song.

'Laughing At The Rain'

An up-tempo song from Paul, whose vocals sound more like him rather than Hugh. However, there is a guitar riff reminiscent of Hugh at the end, but more accomplished. This would appear to be a statement about life and how we react to it. The line, 'The price you pay', seems to be that you can play 'the game of life', but you may have to make sacrifices to get what you want. In the end, Paul is rather positive, and no matter what life throws at him, he will be 'laughing at the rain'.

'This Town'

This is a JJ song and appears to be a gay pride anthem. The lyric suited Paul as, in his teens and 20s, Paul was unsure about his sexuality and would quite often cross-dress. The lyric, 'I don't want to live a lie anymore', is particularly strong. The second half of the song – where he looks to the future – is more upbeat both lyrically and musically, where there can be a world in which love in all its forms is accepted.

The instrumental finale is intriguing, with 'heavy' background feedback and effects, although the whole song has a late sixties 'feel' due to the psychedelic, jangly guitar. It is amongst the more melodic songs that The Stranglers recorded, showcasing vocal harmonies, a gentle keyboard wash and the overall optimistic lyric: 'I want the best for people'.

'Brain Box'

This was the B-side of 'Heaven Or Hell', a fast-paced song from John Ellis which is about our quest for knowledge and understanding. The protagonist of the song is looking for answers and he asks for guidance from 'Caesar's daughter' and a 'Delphic Virgin', who he also has sex with, making it a contradiction in itself. In the end, an 'old timer' tells him that the answers may be within himself – in his 'brain box'.

'Southern Mountains'

This ballad has a great instrumental backing. It's quite basic, with a steady beat, a simple guitar riff and an acoustic guitar solo which is quite beautiful. The singing appears to signify a wistful longing to return to a more simple and pure place. He has been there before but can't seem to get back ('Send me back/Back to Southern Mountains'). It's a desire to get away from modern life. Quite a change from JJ's more aggressive songs.

'Gain Entry To Your Soul'

Here, Paul sings to his high school sweetheart, who apparently has a number of suitors trying to gain her affection: 'If you want me/you know where to call'. Overall, this is a mid-tempo, catchy pop song with some high-pitched backing vocals. Lyrically, this is like a 'grown-up' Goffin and King sixties number, in my opinion, as it is quite 'poppy', with some great 'chunky' guitar and a 'false' ending to keep the listener on their toes. Again from the pen of JJ, this shows that he can write 'pop' songs instead of the darker lyrics.

'Grand Canyon'

This song came from a demo that John had recorded about six years earlier with a singer called Alex Legg. He played it to the band and asked if they should do it. It's about socialism in a way; a ballad about the distance between the poor and the rich and about racial inequality – 'And he don't give a damn/For the mouths he could feed'. The Grand Canyon metaphor is excellent, describing the massive gulf between the rich and poor. Quite an eerie intro graces this song and the track remains unnerving throughout the four minutes plus.

'Wet Afternoon'

This tongue-in-cheek description of a séance forms the basis of one of the best songs on the album by John: 'Hands around a circle/In the candlelight'. There are a lot of film references in John's songs, as he told me: 'I was a film librarian for the British Film Institute for a while and I love films, so a lot of references crop up in my songs. This one is based on *Séance On A Wet Afternoon*, a 1964 film directed by Bryan Forbes'. This is one of The Stranglers' pacey and quirky songs, with some great sound effects. In this regard, it is reminiscent of some of the tracks on *Meninblack*.

'Never See'

A funky track with a bit of slide guitar; the pace here is fired by the keyboards and a Nile Rodgers-style guitar chug. The words seem to convey a comment on racism – 'All they see is a colour of a man's skin' – and we 'never see' what lies behind. The original idea came from JJ and he co-wrote the lyrics with Paul. 'Never See' also shows how the use of words can create confusion and perpetuate biases, which can result in people being trapped in their own mental prisons. On the other hand, the lyrics also suggest that thoughts and words can be used to inspire people and promote a change in attitudes.

'Leave It To The Dogs'

Another John number, explaining – in his words – 'what a shithole London has become and how criminality and anti-social behaviour is making life terrible'. It's gone to the dogs despite the fact that he loves the city. The line, 'Let them pick the bone', would indicate that John feels there is nothing to salvage. Paul thinks it was a good song; however, 'John used to write a lot of songs in D Minor and they all felt rather negative'. To be honest, it *is* a bit depressing.

Other Contemporary Tracks

'Coffee Shop'

Produced by the band and written by JJ, this B-side to 'Heaven Or Hell' has an ethereal intro, with an almost bagpipe-style drone, leading to a mid-tempo pop song. John's guitar is very dominant and is the highlight of the track.

This is about a meeting with a lady at a coffee shop in Amsterdam. Now, in Amsterdam, coffee shops are not just for meeting up and having a coffee. After the decriminalisation of marijuana in Amsterdam in 1976, a coffee shop was the place to go to buy weed (however, in 2023, these 'coffee shops' are only licensed to sell the stuff to Dutch people – not tourists). The part about drugs seems to be indicated by the chorus, which states that 'the judges from the past are no longer sitting' and that 'the guilty of the past are now martyrs'.

As with a lot of Stranglers songs, there is a twist; the line, 'I will have you soon', seems to indicate that the lady we have met is not there for just coffee or weed. Talk about sex and drugs and rock and roll!!

For some reason, the working title for this track was 'Spag Wes', short for Spaghetti Western.

'Vicious Circles'

Again produced by the band, this John-penned song about how people, and women in particular, seem to be drawn to the wrong type of person was another B-side to 'Heaven Or Hell'. We see it in the fact that women correspond with – and even sometimes marry – people in prison. The lyrics, which were written by John and Paul, suggest that they are drawn to violence ('She likes to move in vicious circles'). However, the final lines – 'Now her leather jacket's empty/Like the gun they found beside her' – seem to suggest that the young woman has met her end violently. The song serves as a warning to anyone caught in a similar cycle to seek help and break free from a life of violence. The up-tempo nature of the song masks the dark tone of the lyrics – another Stranglers trademark.

'So Uncool'

The B-side to 'Sugar Bullets', with the many references to drugs like crack and smack, this song would appear to be an anti-drug song in which JJ (who wrote it) expunges his drugs and violent past. The lyrics state, 'I don't see the reason why I'm so uncool'. However, by not 'playing with switchblades' and asserting that 'you can't sell me crack' – in other words, refraining from violence and staying level-headed – he renders himself uncool. 'So Uncool' is a mid-tempo song which contains a great guitar riff from John, but as with the vast majority of the album, the bass is very understated.

'Disappear'

Produced by the band and used as the B-side to 'Heaven Or Hell', this sounds a bit like Simple Minds to my ears (but my wife, who is a Simple Minds fan, says it sounds like The Cure). Either way, it's a great number that shouldn't have been relegated to a B-side, especially when the single in question is extremely hard to get hold of, which is similar to 'Lies And Deception' in that regard.

In another song dealing with sexual orientation, seemingly, the singer is lamenting that he is having no luck with girls, that 'Daddy never taught me how to deal with girls' and that 'When it comes to love, I just disappear'. Because of his inexperience (or sexual orientation), his 'immaculate persuasion' and "cold emotion" let him down.

In 2023, Paul Roberts told me that he thinks it was a song co-written by him and JJ.

About Time (1995)

Personnel:
Paul Roberts: lead vocals, percussion
Jean-Jacques Burnel: bass guitar, vocals
John Ellis: guitar, vocals
Dave Greenfield: keyboards, vocals
Jet Black: drums
Additional personnel:
Nigel Kennedy: violin (on 'Face')
Susie Elliott: vocals (on 'Sinister' and 'And The Boat Sails By')
Chris Winter: harmonica (on 'Golden Boy')
Gavyn Wright: violin (on 'Face', 'Sinister' and 'Still Life')
Wilf Gibson: violin (on 'Face', 'Sinister' and 'Still Life')
Bob Smissen: viola (on 'Face', 'Sinister' and 'Still Life')
Caroline Dale: cello (on 'Face', 'Sinister' and 'Still Life')
Alex Christaki: string arrangements (on 'Face', 'Sinister' and 'Still Life')
Recorded at Rockfield Studios, Monmouth, Parr Street Studios, Liverpool, Westside Studios, London in 1995
Producer: Alan Winstanley and The Stranglers
Engineer: Alan Winstanley
Assistant Engineers: Simon Dawson (Rockfield Studios), Andrea Wright (Parr Street Studios), Lee Phillips (Westside Studios)
Original UK label and catalogue number: When! Records WENCD 001
Released: 15 May 1995 (UK)
Highest chart position: UK: 31
Running time: 44.54
All tracks written by The Stranglers (Paul Roberts, Jean-Jacques Burnel, John Ellis, Dave Greenfield, Jet Black)

All the band were disappointed about the lack of success of *In The Night* and the accompanying singles. However, as a live act, they were still packing them in and were also achieving more success in continental Europe, which would seem to overturn the comments about the band becoming 'Americanised'.

Jet was having a few health problems, too. He was in his mid-fifties and had a couple of periods when he couldn't play. The first was after a gig in Kilburn when a stage light had been placed near a plastic screen and cyanide gas was blown into Jet's face. He was rushed to hospital, and although he rejoined the band the next day, he was eventually flown back home to recover properly. His place was taken by The Damned's Rat Scabies for a few dates before Paul Roberts got the flu and the rest of the dates were cancelled. Jet then dislodged a disc in his back whilst gardening and spent a year in pain as the specialists tried to correct his back. He wasn't allowed to play drums and Tim Bruce and Keith Tobe filled in. Jet did still tour with the band, but only to assure the fans he was still around and to sing (if that's the right word) 'Old Codger'.

There were also moves to get Hugh back into the band, and at one point, Hugh was even asked if he would write for the band (Hugh's own solo career hadn't exactly taken off at this point). Furthermore, it was suggested that a reunion concert be performed with Hugh playing the first half of the show and Paul the second half – to show that the baton had been passed on. It didn't happen.

The band were in prison again – well, not quite. They were in Southwark Street Studios in London, which had formerly been a debtor's prison. They were working on tracks for the next album, the first that would have 'proper' input from Paul, as the songwriting team of Burnel, Ellis and Roberts was still in its infancy. They were also still a great live act, and the *Stranglers V* tour was a great success. The 'V' was to denote the fact that there were now five in the band (the band would use Roman Numerals again in 2006).

The band also had new managers: Sil Willcox and Trevor Long. Sil had been with the band in some capacity or another for 15 years and, therefore, was already a band confidant. Trevor was a businessman who had already managed the likes of Haircut 100 and had served as The Stranglers' Tour Manager during the 1993 tour. Calling themselves Mainstreet Management, they set about rebuilding the band's credibility. The first thing was to stop releasing records on their own label, Psycho, as it was financially draining, and they signed to the Castle Communications subsidiary When!. Castle seemed to be signing up everybody at this time. They had acquired the rights to the Pye Records catalogue, amongst others.

The main problem was getting the new material an airing. Everyone was aware of the band's back catalogue, and everyone wanted to hear it, with only The Stranglers' fans interested in new stuff. And with *In The Night* only shifting around 30,000 copies, something needed to be done. The situation was particularly galling to the new boys, as they were now the dominant writing force within the band. In fact, John Ellis did say at the time that every time he played, he was actually earning more money for Hugh Cornwell than himself and that the plethora of compilations was detracting attention from the 'new' band.

We had two live albums released in the interim: *Saturday Night, Sunday Morning* in 1993, the recording of Hugh's final gig, and *The Stranglers And Friends* in 1995, the recording of the Hugh-less Rainbow gig.

The new album – *About Time* – was recorded early in 1995 and produced by the band and a returning Alan Winstanley, who also engineered and mixed it. It was a return to a more 'organic' rocky sound and is much less technology-dependent than *In The Night*. At first, Jet wasn't particularly happy as he thought it was a backward step, but the rest – and in particular Paul and John – were very happy with it. To capitalise on the fact that the band were seemingly better live than in the studio, the tracks were recorded almost live in the studio with a few overdubs. After lengthy rehearsals, the band had around 20 songs to pick from and 11 made it onto the album.

The cover is a strange one: a blue and black background with the familiar red band logo (with the 'the' back in place) and album title beneath. The image is of a frayed rope held together by a thin thread; I can't help thinking that this was an analogy of the band – just hanging together by a thread.

About Time was released on 15 June 1995 to little fanfare but good reviews. It spent just a single week in the charts, like its predecessor, but at two places higher at number 31. Sales were better, too, doubling the amount sold by *In The Night* worldwide. Only one single was released from the album – 'Lies And Deception' – which was also the title of a two-CD compilation a few years later.

'Golden Boy'

This John-penned song is about celebrities and how undeserving people get turned into celebrities ('Now everyone wants to touch/The Golden Boy'). According to John, 'Only a third of a person's celebrity has to do with talent. Punk rock produced very little great music, but PR makes people into big celebrities'. In essence, it's a cautionary tale about how corrupting power can be and the fickleness of the public. Overall, a solid rocker to begin the album.

'Money'

Another pacey song, this time money and our obsession with it is the focus; it seems to be the 'be all and end all' and we always want more. The line, 'You talk about money, do you need to advertise', denotes the fact that we boast about our wealth. The lyrics also declare the disappointing truth that money is not easy to obtain. According to Paul, who wrote the song, it is based on a story about a financial payout to a severely handicapped person who was asked by a journalist how they felt about all that money. The person says, 'Help me out of my chair/Did you think it was funny talking money'. He is obviously not happy and would trade the money for his health. The whole band put in a good performance here, with equal emphasis on all instruments. Having said that, John plays a nice little solo.

'Face'

A slower track from Paul, with Dave's keyboards being seemingly relegated to a supporting role. Some superb guitar riffs and a great solo from John enhance the whole track. It's also more in keeping with The Stranglers' dark side. The lyrics seem to suggest that the protagonist has been betrayed by someone he loves but still loves them and wants them back. Featured on this track, along with two others, is a string quartet, including Gavyn Wright and Wilfred Gibson from The Penguin Café Orchestra (Wilfred was also a member of the Electric Light Orchestra). Not only a quartet, but punk violinist Nigel Kennedy, a big Stranglers fan himself, puts in an appearance.

'Sinister'

This always went down well live, even though it is a slow – some say 'sinister' – track (which proves that it's a good title). The lyrics portray a woman who drifts through life looking for her next conquest. But beware! She will use us to further her own ends. The string quartet is back and we have Susie Elliott supplying some vocals. The song comes from an R&B-type song that John Ellis came up with. Paul liked it but changed the title, then wrote the lyrics and arrangement.

'Little Blue Lies'

Mr Big is a criminal who bribes people ('He's kicking back and crossing palms'). He's just out of prison ('Mr Big has done his time/He's out today') and seems to be looking to rebuild his empire ('Some old darling's nest egg is just what he needs'). The song reflects on the various guises adopted by the character, highlighting his deceitful mannerisms and his ability to manipulate people's thoughts and actions. The lyrics' theme of dishonesty and deception also reflects the music industry's constant pressure to conform to expectations and the fact that dishonesty has become an accepted practice in society.

'Still Life'

This is the last track to feature the strings. The opening string introduction, at a whopping 1:51 in length, doesn't seem to be connected to the rest of the song. Paul's voice is very emotive on this one, and it has a haunting melody. 'Still Life' looks at emotional pain and heartbreak. The lyrics describe the singer standing naked and vulnerable by the window, watching a storm rage outside and contemplating the possibility of being with someone they once loved. They can't get away from them as they 'see' the person everywhere.

The Kinks pursued this concept in 'No More Looking Back' from their 1975 album *Schoolboys In Disgrace*. This was another collaboration between JJ and Paul, as JJ had the initial idea and wrote the first verse, whilst Paul arranged the song and finished off the lyrics.

'Paradise Row'

This is a John-penned song about when his street was pulled down and he lost his house. Before he joined The Stranglers, John was involved in a bid to stop the M11 link road being built – in fact, he was the Press Officer. However, the bid failed and he lost his house – literally. Mr Ellis is being very clever here with an analogy to the building of the pyramids. The 'poison arrows' are the pyramids of old and the rising new buildings that were replacing the older homes. He is not happy about it: 'It makes my heart bleed'. He bemoans the fact that the displaced residents will have to find somewhere else to live: 'Tell me, Moses, where will your children go?'

'She Gave It All'

Here, we go on a trip to the seedier side of London, Holborn, in fact, with a visit to a prostitute ('red light heaven'). However, after the woman has given herself to him, he still feels unfulfilled ('The search for meaning so profound').

The singer appears to be searching for a sense of belonging. Written by Paul, the music is also more in keeping with the topic, with heavy bass from JJ and a harsh guitar from John.

'Lies And Deception'

This was the only single taken from the album, released in June 1995 on When! Records (WENX 1007). It reached number 94 in its two-week stay in the charts. It was released as a cassette and a two-CD set. CD1 had 'Swim' and 'Cool Danny' as additional tracks, whilst CD2 had 'Kiss The World Goodbye' and 'Bed Of Nails'. Like 'Disappear' on the 'Heaven Or Hell' single, none of these additional tracks have been issued on an album.

Some jazzy Spanish guitar adorns the middle of the track, probably due to the drummer's Jazz upbringing, as this song is the ONLY Stranglers track that was written solely by their stalwart drummer. In fact, the whole song sounds as though it could be played in one of those dingy jazz dives we see on television.

The song came from a couple of episodes in Jet's life where he had heard conversations over the phone when the receiver had been left off the hook. The lyrics showed that Jet had, over the years, become a little more poetic, unlike the early days when, according to the band, his lyrics sounded like business letters.

'Lucky Finger'

Another John-penned song, this time about fate and luck. You can just be tootling along when the big finger of fate touches you. The National Lottery advertisement, with the big finger and 'it could be you', might have been in the back of his mind. The singer had given up on success ('And abandoned all hope'), but if success does come his way, 'I'll raise my face and give thanks to the heavens'. Overall, another mid-tempo song which would have made a good 'pop' single.

'And The Boat Sails By'

Another film-based song from John, this time on the 1983 Fellini film *And The Ship Sails On*, about how life passes you by. It is also a stunning description of the beauty of the sea in all its forms, and the lyrics perfectly capture these elements with lines like, 'And the boast sails by/under crimson skies' and 'Cool wind blow me home to you'. It takes the listener on a journey of serene beauty. Dave brings out the steel drum sound on the keyboards to demote sunny climes and we have Susie back in the background.

Other Contemporary Tracks

'Swim'

We have more keyboards out front here than on any other track on *About Time*, except 'Still Life'. This was released as an additional track on CD1 of the 'Lies And Deception' single. John's echo-y guitar work adds atmosphere to this song by Paul, underpinned excellently by JJ's bass.

'Cool Danny'

A powerful intro sets us off, with drums, followed by bass, then guitar and finally keyboards. Musically, much like The Stranglers of old, this is almost like a rock 'n' roll number with a hint of Mod courtesy of Dave's Hammond Organ. This was the second additional track on 'Lies And Deception' CD1. With lyrics by JJ and Paul, the original idea came from JJ.

'Kiss The World Goodbye'

Released as an additional track on CD2 of the 'Lies And Deception' single, this is a very rare track. This is a rhythmic song with touches of Hugh Cornwell-like guitar.

'Bed Of Nails'

This was the second additional track on 'Lies And Deception' CD2.

Written In Red (1997)

Personnel:
Paul Roberts: lead vocals, percussion
Jean-Jacques Burnel: bass guitar, vocals
John Ellis: guitar, vocals
Dave Greenfield: keyboards, vocals
Jet Black: drums
Additional personnel:
Dave Billow: vocals
Recorded at Parr Street Studios, The Greenhouse, Gemini Studios, Intimate Studios in Summer 1996
Producer: Andy Gill and The Stranglers
Additional Production: Cenzo Townshend
Engineers: Jock Loveband, Peter Schweir, Pete Woodruff, Chris Madden
Assistant Engineers: Cenzo Townsend, Mitsou Tate, Andrea Wright
Original UK label and catalogue number: When! Records WENCD 009
Released: 27 January 1997 (UK)
Highest chart position: UK: 52
Running time: 40.51
All tracks written by The Stranglers (Paul Roberts, Jean-Jacques Burnel, John Ellis, Dave Greenfield, Jet Black), except 'Summer In The City' by John Sebastian, Mark Sebastian, Steve Boone

The relative failure of *About Time* led the band to reconsider their approach. The attempt to go back to the old sound hadn't worked, so perhaps they should go for a more contemporary vibe; we were getting close to the new millennium, and the band were still in the 70s, or so it seemed. The new 'rock' music was 'grunge' and 'garage', which would probably have suited the band 20 years earlier, so they decided that they would keep with their own brand of songs whilst at the same time updating it slightly. To that end, they brought in Andy Gill, who, after his work with Gang Of Four, was a more experimental producer. The problem was, however, the band themselves.

According to John Ellis, JJ and Dave were still pretty much in limbo; JJ, in particular, didn't seem interested in writing much. When the band came together to rehearse and trial songs for the next album, Paul and John had about a dozen songs each, whilst JJ had a few ideas which he played on an acoustic guitar. This meant that the majority of songs would be originated by the two newbies. JJ said in 2014 that 'it had nothing to do with me apart from one or two songs' and 'I had given up in the band; it wasn't a band anymore, just John and Paul and a guy with Pro Tools' (Pro Tools is a digital audio workstation used for music creation and production).

Paul was both annoyed and pleased; annoyed because he and John were left to 'carry the can', as he put it, but happy because they had more artistic control. Dave was feeling a bit marginalised as his contributions were relegated to the background. He said at the time that Paul and John were bringing completed songs into the rehearsals and wanted them done as they had been written, but in the Hugh days, when someone brought in a song, it acted as a catalyst for the band to contribute their ideas. Jet was the one original who had more enthusiasm for the new album, although he was becoming more grumpy (if that were possible) and prone to strops.

The album was recorded throughout the summer of 1996 and the release was held back to January 1997 to avoid it getting lost in the Christmas rush. The album was recorded differently in that Andy Gill had each band member record their parts separately in the studio with no other member there. Unfortunately, the main strength of The Stranglers is playing as a band and this allows them to make suggestions as they go along. Almost every member of the band was against this, but it was the way Gill wanted to record it.

Written In Red was launched at Euro Disney in December 1996. The band's management transported selected fans and media people for what they called a 'Saturday Night Special' at the theme park just outside Paris, where the band played the whole of the new album – except, for some reason, 'Wonderful Land' – and a selection of hits. The event had no effect on sales of the album, and according to JJ, the band were 'not on form'.

Finally released on 27 January 1997, it was the poorest performing album (chart-wise) so far, hitting only number 52, the first studio album by the band not to reach the top 40 and, like the preceding two Stranglers Mark II albums, spent only one week in the charts. Sil Willcox said, prior to the release, that the band needed to sell 100,000 copies of the album and have a top 20 single. Neither was forthcoming.

The change in style was also reflected on the fairly abstract sleeve, showcasing an odd mixture of water, fluid and blood. What was different, however, was that the album cover did not feature the familiar Stranglers logo for the first time since *La Folie* in 1981.

Only one single was taken from the album: 'In Heaven She Walks'.

'Valley Of The Birds'

A combined effort here, written after playing a festival in New Zealand. The band used to take to the stage to this number during the live shows at this time, as the bird song gave an eerie (almost Hitchcockian) vibe. JJ had the initial idea and wrote the first verse. John added a superb riff and Paul wrote the lyrics.

When the song kicks in, it's Paul at his best. The sound is very Stranglers-ish with quite a decent rhythm, underpinned with a bit of evil in the vocals, not forgetting the keyboard backing. Using, as a metaphor, a soldier called Ray in the Vietnam War, the song explores war (obviously) and escapism – the lyrics infer that he wants to fly away.

'In Heaven She Walks'

This was the only single taken from the album. Released on 3 February 1997 on When! Records (WENX 1018), it was available on two CDs. The first CD included a live version of 'Golden Brown' from 1995 and an extended version of 'In Heaven She Walks', whereas the second CD had live versions of 'Grip' and 'Something Better Change' (also from 1995). In its single week in the charts, it reached the not-so-dizzying heights of number 86, and it would be the last single for seven years. A song from Paul, it's extremely catchy with some jangly guitar and as strong as anything the band had released for years. It's criminal that this wasn't a hit, but not really surprising as The Stranglers were not being played on the radio these days (apart from 'Oldies' stations).

The song is about being obsessed with a person you keep running into in different places. The singer is so obsessed with this person that they can pick them out in a crowd. It is also suggested that the person is 'too' perfect to be real.

'In A While'

Quite a jaunty but moody song; this is the one track on the album that sounds 'European'. The Stranglers have a penchant for disguising dark subjects with up-tempo music. JJ came up with the idea and the chorus while the lyrics and arrangement were by Paul. He wrote the lyrics on a tablecloth at a Chinese restaurant in Liverpool whilst on a bender with John Ellis, Nigel Kennedy and a couple of others. Paul states that Andy Gill was very key to this track: 'We played around with ambient guitars and mixed the idea at his place', he told me in 2023. The dark subject is the fleeting nature of life and wanting to find one's place in the world. The singer feels that there is something missing in their life but is unsure of what it is.

'Silver Into Blue'

Traditional rock, unsuited to the band's more trademark sound, greets us here. The only hint of The Stranglers is Paul's voice. Paul, who wrote the song, tells me that it is about a 'personal drug experience in an aeroplane ... not recommended to anyone to partake in at that height. I originally titled it 'Tangled Up In Blue', but, of course, another lesser-known song by a certain Mr Zimmerman had taken that title'. It would appear that the lyrics are a metaphor for being at peace and appreciating the beauty of nature, but we might stagnate and, therefore, must venture out.

'Blue Sky'

Some plodding percussion adds to the psychedelic vibe here, with hints of Gary Numan and some strings courtesy of Dave Greenfield's keyboards. Paul wrote this song for Marian Shepherd, who ran the Stranglers Information Service (SIS) until its demise in 1997. He says: 'we were very close and she had some worrying health issues back then'. This song discusses the feelings of loss and regret, not taking chances when they cropped up (we've all been there) and addresses the insecurities that live within us all.

'Here'

Quite a dark piece but quite poppy, this has a sound not unlike a Bond film theme, especially with Paul's voice and the deep, twangy guitar. Another Paul-penned song, which he says was inspired by 'The Gift' by the Velvet Underground. There is an overall feeling of being trapped in a situation that is causing distress and wanting something more satisfying in life.

'Joy De Viva'

A song from John, the title is a pun on the phrase 'joie de vivre', which means 'the enjoyment of life'. This is the exact opposite of the French phrase and likens the enjoyment of life to a woman ('Joy De Viva'). 'The song is about losing your life force', according to John when we spoke in 2023. 'I was depressed as I'd lost my house' (see 'Paradise Row'). 'In fact, a lot of artists write in a state of depression'. It has a soaring melody and a chorus that wouldn't be out of place in any pop song in the 1980s. However, this was the 1990s and tracks like this, like quite a few on this album, sounded a bit anachronistic.

'Miss You'

Again, like 'Silver Into Blue', this is another delve into more traditional rock music; its insistent beat gets the toe-tapping. Lyrically, the song appears to be about a relationship that has ended, but we still miss the person we are apart from and hope that one day we can move on. Paul thinks he wrote the lyrics, whilst John thinks it may have been a song by JJ.

'Daddy's Riding The Range'

Another John-penned song, this time it's for his daughter. He is contemplating his own mortality (no doubt the depression talking again) and wants his daughter to have a good image of him. He, therefore, imagines himself dressed in a toy cowboy suit ('That his mother bought for him'), riding the Wild West. Paul's voice is 'lighter' on this track, as though he is trying to be more friendly; after all, he is singing to a child. 'John's original song was beautiful', Paul tells me, '...more acoustic-based ... Andy Gill took it in a totally different direction, which was how it ended up – brilliant. I added certain melodies (especially the bridge and chorus). I, Andy and John worked through to put it all together'.

'Summer In The City' (Sebastian, Sebastian. Boone)

John Ellis thinks it was Andy Gill's idea to record this song, as the band seem to do well with covers. John remembers, 'We used a lot of effects on the guitar'. Paul also remembers that Andy, along with himself and John, arranged and structured the song. Both this and 'Blue Sky' had been put together by samples that Paul had sorted out. He then remixed them in the studio. Originally a hit for The Lovin' Spoonful in 1966, it had been covered quite recently (1994) by Joe Cocker, who had a decent hit with it in Europe. It has been covered by Cocker, Styx, Isaac Hayes, BB King, and Eels, but no mention of The Stranglers.

Most people dislike this track, even though all the band members thought that it was very contemporary sounding. However, I must stick my beak in here. This is one of my favourite tracks by The Stranglers, mainly because of its quirkiness and the percussion. When I first played this album, *Summer In The City* hit me like a brick in the face and I played it incessantly for days.

'Wonderful Land'

Here, there is a nice use of the wah-wah pedal on John's guitar, with Dave's keyboards very much in the background. This song appears to be a nostalgic look at past times; the 'sepia memory' refers to old photographs which are sepia in colour – we should learn from the past. Again, Paul thinks it's a John Ellis song, whilst John seems to think it was either JJ or Paul.

Coup De Grace (1998)

Personnel:
Paul Roberts: vocals
Jean-Jacques Burnel: bass guitar, vocals
John Ellis: guitar
Dave Greenfield: keyboards, programming, vocals
Jet Black: drums
Additional personnel:
Lisa George: vocals (on 'You Don't Think That What You've Done Is Wrong')
Lizzie Deane: vocals (on 'You Don't Think That What You've Done Is Wrong')
Recorded at Funny Bunny Studios, London, Matrix Studios, London between 1997 and 1998
Producer: The Stranglers, David M. Allen
Engineers: David M. Allen, Chris Jarrett, Matt Hay
Assistant Engineers: Clare, Ben, Neil
Original UK label and catalogue number: Eagle Records EAGCD042
Released: 26 October 1998 (UK)
Highest chart position: UK: 171
Running time: 42.46
All tracks written by The Stranglers (Paul Roberts, Jean-Jacques Burnel, John Ellis, Dave Greenfield, Jet Black)

We had less than two years to wait until the new Stranglers album, and this time, the band were signed to Eagle Records who, like Castle Communications, specialised in signing 'retro' bands like Deep Purple, ELP, Yes, Jethro Tull and Status Quo, to name but a few. In fact, we had even less than that because *Friday The Thirteenth*, a superb live album – recorded on Friday 13 June 1997 – had been released with an accompanying DVD. Also, David Buckley's excellent book *No Mercy – The Authorised And Uncensored Biography* was published by Hodder & Stoughton. Moreover, the band were busy live – as usual. In May, they entertained the troops in Bosnia, and in November, they played in The Falkland Islands. The travels to entertain the troops influenced the writing of the band's 14th studio album *Coup de Grace*, released on 26 October 1998 and produced by the band and engineer David M Allen.

According to John Ellis, it was JJ who wrote all of the tracks on the album. He also returns to singing some of the lead vocals by providing the lead voice on four of the ten tracks. Dave also returned to the microphone for one track, leaving Paul Roberts to do the other five. The topics covered by the songs include failed relationships, religious conflicts, the devastation caused by war, and, in JJ's words, 'life in general'.

Coup De Grace holds the record (no pun intended) for being the worst-performing studio album the band released, only reaching number 171 in the UK. The cover showcases a golden image of a religious icon and the band logo in red on a black background. The lyrics include a short description explaining (a bit) what the songs are about. This was the final album to feature John Ellis, whose writing for the album was ignored, as he explained to me in 2023. 'I wrote 12 songs for that album', he says. 'The producer came to my studio and said that they were fantastic. He then took them to Cambridge, where JJ and Dave were working, and none of them were used. In the end, they were recorded and released on my solo album *Infinity Drive*'.

There were no singles taken from *Coup De Grace*, and to date, it is the *only* Stranglers studio album from which no singles were released.

'God Is Good'

The opening track is an electronic chant with the whole band singing (although it is thought of as a Dave lead vocal). The lyrics to 'God Is Good' are a damning comment on religious fundamentalism, particularly violence and bigotry. The repetition of the phrase 'God is good' indicates the thoughtless, dogmatic repetition that is often heard in religion. The words, 'This was my land, now it's yours/But when we're gone, it will always be gone', indicate that religious conflict can be rooted in land ownership and territorial disputes. Furthermore, the last two lines about slitting the throat of the infidel and killing the children are JJ voicing his disgust about the then-current conflict in Algeria, where in the previous four years, over 90,000 people – in the main youngsters – were murdered by having their throats cut. It is a powerful commentary on the dangers of blind faith and religious extremism.

'You Don't Think That What You've Done Is Wrong'

This is the 'relationship breakup' song. The singer's partner has obviously done something wrong that they don't think is wrong. It involves trust and the singer feels that they have been betrayed. The loyalty they have shown doesn't appear to have been reciprocated. I can't help feeling that this is a deeply personal song by JJ, reflecting something that happened in his life. A mid-tempo 'poppy' song sung by JJ.

'Tonight'

'Tonight' is a song about getting away from the seriousness and responsibilities of life, and if things are getting a bit – er – heavy ('tricks the Gods play on man'), just talking it through. The protagonist used to mull things over by staying up and smoking pot, but now that he has matured, he needs to talk to someone. But they can still 'get shit-faced and talk rubbish'. Overall, this is a slower song with Paul singing introspectively and 'in his cups' (i.e. drunk, inebriated).

'Jump Over My Shadow'

This song concerns injustice, hypocrisy and greed. In fact, it's best described using the notes that were published with the album's lyrics: 'Some things are worth going that extra mile for, worth fighting for, and some things aren't. Unfortunately, values have been turned upside down in recent years and hype and false Gods dictate our thinking and common sense is scorned'. A quarter of a century after these lyrics were written, things haven't changed. Paul sings this pacier number, which is, like many of the tracks on *Coup De Grace*, very far removed from the typical Stranglers sound.

'Miss You'

This would seem to be a reworked version of the track of the same name from *Written In Red*. 'You were a pain in the arse – and now I miss you' sums it up pretty well – we've all been there. A relationship ended, but the person you have split from completes you in some way. As the album note says: 'Can't' live with them, can't live without them'. JJ is on lead vocals here; it's a very plaintive number, with JJ singing maybe at the top of his range. In fact, it's almost heading into 'La Folie' territory.

'Coup De Grace (S-O-S)'

A very dark and depressing song about someone who is at the end of their tether and wants to be put out of their misery. Sadly, they haven't got the strength and are asking for someone to apply the 'coup de grace' and end it all for them. However, JJ has inserted (if that's the right word) a little bit of innuendo (again, sorry for the choice of words): 'O Lord I'm on my knees – save our holes'. Is he hinting at anal sex here? Dave's organ is dominant on the title track, which is sung by Paul – that is very much *not* a bad thing. If it was faster paced, it would be more typical of The Stranglers of old.

'In The End'

This song, at a mid-pace and with Dave supplying a stringed (synthesiser) background, talks about life's journey and experiences and asks a philosophical question: would we change our life's journey if we could see the future? The answer is that we make mistakes because we have free will. We hold our destiny in our own hands. The song also ponders whether we ask too many philosophical questions about life when we should just go with the flow. As the liner note says: 'What is destiny? What is free will? What is fate? ... fuck knows'. There are just too many unanswerable questions in life.

'No Reason'

Another slow number sung by Paul, 'No Reason' is a lament about a failed relationship ending without an apparent reason. There is confusion and longing for the relationship not to end. The singer lists his flaws, which seem to have contributed to the breakup, and begs for another chance. It is a search for the answers as to why it has happened – nothing happens for no reason.

It can be said that the whole album appears to be a lot 'slower' than most others by the band. This could be one of the reasons why it didn't do well.

Stranglers fans expect something gritty and up-tempo in the main. But then, the subject matter doesn't exactly lend itself to 'happy' music.

'Known Only Unto God'

This is JJ's tribute to the sacrifice of soldiers who died in wars and were buried in unknown graves. The lyrics tell us of a young man who was loved by someone but died in a foreign land and was only known to God. The album note tells us: 'There is a cemetery on the Falkland Islands for the Argentinians, many of whom died with no ID. On the crosses, there is only this inscription. Here there lies – under southern skies/a young man loved by someone – known unto God'. The atmospheric opening brings to mind the wind blowing across the killing fields. JJ's vocals are straightforward, with a simple and evocative musical backing. Halfway through, John Ellis plays a very thoughtful and beautiful guitar break.

'The Light'

'The Light' touches upon life being predestined and the powerful impact of darkness. It also alludes to an event that left a deep impression, very probably a romantic or sexual experience. The chorus implies that darkness can provide some peace of mind. Sometimes, it's better to accept the unknown and embrace darkness as part of life. The song ends with an air of acceptance that whatever happens, it's too late to change now. The slight tempo change in the chorus lifts this song, which is sung by Paul. Also of note is John Ellis playing what sounds like a mandolin in the background. To be honest, John's work on this album was just about the best he'd ever done with The Stranglers – it was a fitting swansong for him.

Laid Black (2001)

Personnel:
Paul Roberts: lead vocals, percussion
Jean-Jacques Burnel: bass guitar, vocals
Baz Warne: guitar, harmonica, vocals
Dave Greenfield: keyboards, guitar, vocals
Jet Black: drums, percussion
Recorded at ARC Studios, Bath in 2001
Producer: Max Bisgrove
Engineers: Max Bisgrove, Henry Skinner
Original UK label and catalogue number: Zen Records ZEN 00312
Released: 2001
Highest chart position: n/a
Running time: 28:29
All tracks written by The Stranglers (Paul Roberts, Jean-Jacques Burnel, Dave Greenfield, Jet Black, Hugh Cornwell, John Ellis)
Tracklisting: 'Walk On By', 'Let Me Down Easy', 'Southern Mountains', 'Cruel Garden', 'European Female', 'Still Life', 'Always The Sun', 'Face', 'Strange Little Girl', 'Princess Of The Streets', 'Golden Brown', 'Old Codger', 'Mony Mony', 'In The End'

This is almost certainly the first Stranglers recording the new recruit Baz Warne played on. He remembers thinking: 'If we never recorded anything again, I'd always have this record as proof that I had actually been in the Stranglers ... funny how some things stick in your mind'. The band had just done the convention at Brean Sands in Burham on Sea as a sort of introduction of Baz to the fans and played an acoustic set for the very first time. Apparently, it went down very well. It's a representation of the convention set, hence the inclusion of 'Old Codger' and 'Mony Mony'.

The album was recorded over two to three days and was recorded as live as possible. The band selected songs for the acoustic gig that would either work in an acoustic 'unplugged' format or were acoustic-style songs anyway, for example, 'Cruel Garden' and 'European Female'. Baz remembers:

> To be honest, I'd only been in the band around a year and my feet had barely touched the ground, and I was still living up in Sunderland with my first wife and kids. We hadn't even started working on material for what became *Norfolk Coast*, which was to come quite soon afterwards ... so maybe we did this as a kind of stop-gap and as a result of the favourable press we got for the acoustic show we'd done.
>
> Not long after this, I, JJ and Dave lived together for eight months, writing and getting to know each other, with Jet, who lived nearby, coming in most days and Paul commuting in from London probably three or four days a week. It was a great time.

Norfolk Coast (2004)

Personnel:
Paul Roberts: lead vocals, percussion
Jean-Jacques Burnel: bass guitar, vocals
Baz Warne: guitar, vocals
Dave Greenfield: keyboards, vocals
Jet Black: drums, percussion
Additional personnel:
Jon Sevink: violin solo (on 'Sanfte Kuss')
Recorded at Good Luck Studios, London in 2003
Producer: Mark Wallis, David Ruffy, Peter Glenister
Engineers: Mark Wallis, David Ruffy
Pre-production Engineers: Louie Nicastro, Max Bisgrove
Original UK label and catalogue number: Liberty/EMI Records 7243 5 96951 2 9
Released: 16 February 2004 (UK)
Highest chart position: UK: 70, France: 142
Running time: 40.03
All tracks written by The Stranglers (Paul Roberts, Jean-Jacques Burnel, Baz Warne, Dave Greenfield, Jet Black)

We had to wait until well into the new millennium for the next 'proper' studio album, although in 2002, we had the *Laid Black* album, which was a self-released acoustic album. There was also the live album *5 Live 01*.

In the meantime, quite a few changes had taken place. The band had a new guitarist in Baz Warne, John Ellis having left in 2000, and the band had re-signed with EMI Records. Also, in 2001, EMI reissued all the band's albums recorded for the label, with new sleeve notes and bonus tracks. This was masterminded by Steve Woof, who was the Head of Range Marketing at EMI and is listed in the liner notes for the reissues as 'Our Man At EMI'. He was also the Project Coordinator for *Norfolk Coast* and the next album *Suite XIV*. Speaking in 2023, Steve told me:

> The reissues idea and concept were the brainchild of filmmaker Alan G. Parker ('Who Killed Nancy?', 'Hello Quo'). He was the main guy, and he had all the knowledge ... We went to Abbey Road and played all the tracks and extra tracks for the band. One or two (mainly live tracks) were rejected by the band as, in their opinion, they weren't good enough. But as Project Manager, I made it happen. I co-ordinated all the press etc.

Speaking to John in 2023, he explained why he left the band.

> I was mentally quite unwell and there was a lot of stuff going on. The Stranglers are a dark force and it's not easy being around them. On the last tour I did, I was only getting two hours' sleep ... I wasn't sacked from the

band, although I knew that JJ wanted me out. I was actually offered a great job in the burgeoning internet world.

It wasn't all negative for him, as he explains: 'Overall, it was good and bad. We did some great gigs and I went to places I would never have gone to. I got wages for ten years and got some of my songs recorded'.

The newcomer, Baz Warne, was born Barry Warne on 25 March 1964 in Sunderland (he is an avid supporter of Sunderland's football team). In 1995, his band Smalltown Heroes supported The Stranglers on tour and, when John left, he was invited to audition and was successful, joining the band in April. The band immediately went off to play in Kosovo. As time went on, Baz became more and more important within the band, becoming – with JJ – the main songwriter and co-lead vocalist when Paul Roberts left.

As we saw with *Coup De Grace*, JJ had begun to reassert his influence on the band, as he said in 2014: 'At one point we were a bit lost direction-wise and musically. I hadn't contributed much, and suddenly, I had this revival of interest'. In 1999, JJ took himself off to the village of Holme-next-the-Sea in a secluded part of Norfolk and, inspired by the scenery and his thoughts, wrote the songs that would become the basis for the album, with the title track and 'Big Thing Coming' being written first. JJ states that after three months, everything had turned round both for him and the band. The album was preceded in February by 'Big Thing Coming', which returned the band to the Singles charts. This was followed in April by 'Long Black Veil', which also charted.

Just a couple of months after Baz joined, he and JJ formed a songwriting partnership and worked on new songs for the next couple of years before recording them. The songs were played live first, meaning they didn't need to spend much time in the studio. Steve Woof remembers: 'It was good fun and they were responsive to ideas and Paul was up for anything'.

Dave's trademark keyboard sound – which some call 'swirling' – came back into the musical mix and it was a definite return to form for the band. It also returned them to the album charts, albeit at number 70 (but was the best showing since *Written In Red*).

The album's cover showed the band on Hunstanton Beach in a portrait taken in 2003 by American photographer Harrison Funk, with the album title in white and band logo in red. It was used for the 'Big Thing Coming' single, and a silhouette of the band image was used for the 'Long Black Veil' single.

A short film based on the album was released in 2006. Directed by Robin Bextor (father of Sophie Ellis-Bextor) and featuring Nicholas Ball, Susannah York and JJ, it won a number of awards.

'Norfolk Coast'

This was the track that kickstarted the idea of the album. Returning to a rockier and more song-led record, its roots lay in unrest and a yearning for validity again, according to Baz.

There'd been a lot of turbulence in the band prior to Baz's joining with one thing and another, and JJ, in particular, was very troubled by it. The reaction to *Coup De Grace* hurt JJ very much. The album had been JJ's attempt to re-assert his influence in the band, and although his intentions were honest, it didn't really work and this left him even more directionless. This is why he took himself off to Norfolk and came up with this track, which Baz states is 'a gem ... and, in my opinion, Mark III's best-recorded highlight by some margin ... although it changed direction a couple of times and needed quite a bit of TLC before we found it'. It started out as a downbeat acoustic track and according (again) to Baz:

> Jet and I remember not being particularly keen on it at first ... but as we worked on it, we realised the best way to deal with it was to kick it heftily up the arse ... and when JJ almost angrily played the bass intro one day, saying 'why can't we just fucking do it like this?!', we knew we had something.
>
> I tweaked the guitar chords a bit ... adding some dissonance to the end of the vocal passages, worked a solo out and cranked the gain levels right up, and Dave came up with some great filtered sequences which open the track.

The band recorded it as an experiment in two days; when they received the track after being mixed, Baz, in particular, was pleased:

> I remember being completely blown away ... that fucking bass was back and it sounded like The Stranglers again ... a new, sleek and somehow more modern-sounding Stranglers ... but undoubtedly us. There were a lot of excited phone calls that day, I remember, and we realised that we had a direction for the album to take ... still one of my favourite tracks ... new or old.

The intro grabs you by the short and curlies with Dave's keys and the pounding, growling bass, which drives the song along at a great pace.

'Big Thing Coming'

Another song that came from JJ's stay in Norfolk and the 'big thing coming' could be related to the discovery of Seahenge, a 4000-year-old timber circle that was found in 1998. They hoped that it would answer numerous questions about the Bronze Age. The other 'big thing coming' could have been the new start to the band's fortunes: 'There is a new time coming/We're gonna have to change'.

Baz was sifting through some ideas they'd recorded and came across 30 seconds of music with a great hook. JJ suggested that Baz play around with it until the band reconvened. Baz added what he calls a 'T. Rex guitar riff'. The song adhered to the same rhythm throughout the song and Baz has a strong memory from the recording: 'My one abiding memory of recording it was seeing Dave's face when he heard the arpeggio keys coming back at him through the studio monitors for the first time ... he turned to me beaming and said, "I'm back!"'.

This was the first single taken from the album, released at the same time (February 2004) on Liberty Records 548 0690. It was released as a CD single, with 'I Don't Agree' and a live version of 'Tucker's Grave' recorded at the Shepherd's Bush Empire. Also, if you inserted the CD into your PC, you could watch an EPK (Electronic Press Kit) video of 'Big Thing Coming'. The single reached number 31 in the UK Singles chart. CD2 had a re-recording of 'Peaches' as 'Peaches 2004'.

'Long Black Veil'

This is the first Stranglers song on the album written by Baz. He wasn't in a good place at this time. His marriage was failing and the lyrics reflect that: 'Life was good for a short while' then 'Sun went down never to rise'. As the lyrics are quite down, Baz decided to offset it with the upbeat singalong chorus. A lot of work went into the song, exemplified by the numerous chord changes and call-and-response guitar. Dave's piano part is exquisite and Jet plays the verses on the sidestick (this method of playing is where you hold the drumstick flat against the snare drumhead and tap the rim) before powering into the chorus, while JJ's bass weaves through and carries the song along. Paul puts in a great vocal and Baz describes the song as a 'great band effort'.

The track was chosen as the second single, which pleased Baz on a personal level, although it only reached number 51 on the UK charts. Again issued as a CD single (Liberty Records 7243 5 48906 2 8) in April 2004, it contained the Radio Edit of 'Long Black Veil', a previously unreleased new song 'Life's Too Short', 'Waltzinblack' (it was being used in a TV advert for Vodaphone at the time) and an extended album version of 'Long Black Veil'.

'I've Been Wild'

Baz came up with the riff on this track, and for some reason, he thought that he should write a song about JJ from JJ's point of view. After some initial reservations, JJ warmed to the idea. With an opening lyric of 'There were times when I did things I shouldn't have done', it's got JJ to a tee. Initially, the song was a lot faster, but after the decision was made to slow the track down a bit, it came together better. Baz says:

> People love fast songs, but if they're not treated right, they can just blend into a dirge. The riffs and power come out more if the tempo is right and not steaming away. I think a lot of Stranglers songs have suffered from this, particularly live when the blood's up and we're charging into the fray. The riffs suffer, and this band are big on riffs.

Singer Paul Roberts likes the song in particular and gives a superb performance.

'Dutch Moon'

This song has the distinction of being the first song that Baz Warne wrote for The Stranglers, as he states: 'I'd been with them for ten weeks and thought I better try something. All I had was the title'. This was from when he looked out of a tour bus window in Holland, where he was touring at the time with The Smalltown Heroes. He continues, '[It was] in the memory banks for about five years until it became a sort of skewed love song. Sometimes, you hear people saying that a song wrote itself, and that's the case with this one; the lyrics came in about 15 minutes'. Jet, in particular, was complimentary about the song and Baz thinks the band were expecting a punky thrash.

Sadly, it wasn't included in the first batch of songs recorded for the album, but a few weeks later, it was mentioned and JJ, along with Dave and Jet, added their bits and the song came to life. The song was recorded in almost one take. Baz adds: 'It's a lovely song. No fat and great individual playing from everyone'.

'Lost Control'

JJ brought this to the band almost completed, but it was difficult to record, and apparently, there are a number of demo versions of 'Lost Control' in existence, all of which are different. JJ was commenting on his own unease at the urban decay that was happening around London; to match the anger of the lyrics, the band add the power that the words required. The squealing car brakes during the rant in the middle were done on the guitar. Baz remembers that it was a great live track: 'When we played it live, we got the sub-bass really cooking in an attempt to make people crap themselves'.

'Into The Fire'

Baz is celebrating party culture here and wanted to write a song about being as hedonistic as possible. He tells me: 'The opening line, "I need a woman like a stag needs a hat rack", was particularly intended to get people's backs up, and it did ... one writer called us misinformed sexist pigs ... mission accomplished then'. The song suffers a little from excessive overdubbed guitar, and although the licks were intrinsic to the recording, it couldn't be replicated live and so is the only track on the entire album that the band have never performed live.

'Tucker's Grave'

I'm going to let Baz Warne tell the story of this song:

> Somewhere between the villages of Norton St Philip and Faulkland in Northeast Somerset is the cider house known as Tuckers Grave. I won't waste much time here trying to describe it because no words can do it justice unless you've been there. There isn't a bar, no music, and nine times out of ten, your mobile won't get a signal. Up until 25 years ago, if you

wanted a piss, you went outside and did it up against the wall … and that included the women too. It's a celebration in the dying art of spontaneous conversation … and if you haven't got any, stay at home. The place is alive with character and characters, the cider is lethal and the landlady's tongue is as sharp as a cutthroat razor. The locals play Skittles in an alley at the back and are brought big plates of homemade cheddar, bread and pickles after the game … I was carried out once after 'accidentally' drinking seven pints … I was in bed for two days … In other words, it's fucking fantastic.

We spent many a happy hour there during this time. Getting to know each other and just relaxing into what we were doing … and JJ and I developed an interest in the history of the place. Edward Tucker was tied to a tree stump on the crossroads outside the pub after hanging himself at the very farm we now call home sometime in the latter half of the 18th century [actually 1747] … he couldn't be given a Christian burial because he'd taken his own life and that was against the law … so they just trussed him up and left him to rot. The local wildlife had a field day and the locals used his corpse as target practice … nice. His story is included in a booklet on the mantle in the pub's living room for all to see, and after reading it one night, we decided to write about it. I remember JJ calling me on his way home one weekend and asking me to 'write this down' … he had quite a lot of the lyrics in his head and between us, down the phone, we came up with the rest. I'd been messing around with open tunings on the guitar and after putting it into DADGAD, came up with the rolling chord sequence. I've had a lot of people over the years asking me how it was done because they can't play it … and you can't in regular tuning … We wanted to make it trancy and atmospheric and Dave's keys really gave it that slant … also, Jet syncopated the snare drum … building it very slowly up into a spooky march of the dead … Paul absolutely sang the shit out of it, and to my mind, this is one of his best-ever recorded performances … I love this track.

In 1999, the band's manager Sil Willcox bought the farmhouse in which Tucker died, Charlton Farm, which would house the band's rehearsal and recording studios.

'I Don't Agree'

'I Don't Agree' appears to have come together organically. JJ started the process off with the bass riff, Baz joined in with the opening guitar riff and Dave supplied some fast keyboard runs, which led up to the chorus. In fact, the whole song was put together in one afternoon. When first released, the band played it live and Baz remembers it went down very well. The 'jangly' guitar at the end was inspired by The Byrds. According to Baz, Paul supplied a great vocal; in fact, he says 'he sang very well on the whole album'.

The lines, 'You haven't been straight with me' and 'You say you're the good guy/But you sound just like the bad one', would seem to infer that JJ had a gripe with someone. Many people at the time thought that this song was a dig at Hugh Cornwell, but in October 2023, JJ assured me that it wasn't. He was keeping pretty schtum about the target, though.

'Sanfte Kuss'

This is the first song that Baz and JJ wrote together. When they got together at JJ's in Cambridge in mid-2000 to see if they could write as a duo, the first thing that JJ played to Baz was the bass parts, and he already had the lyrics. Baz picked up on the vibe – an intimate club setting – and the song was written in a couple of hours. There are no keyboards, just guitar, bass, drums played by brushes and a violin courtesy of The Levellers' Jon Sevink. When the band played it live, Dave used to play rhythm guitar on it.

'Sanfte Kuss' is German for 'A Gentle Kiss'. There are three verses, all sung in different languages – German, French and finally English – where we discover that all JJ really wants is to fuck ... surprise surprise.

'Mine All Mine'

Paul's sole contribution to the album writing-wise, but one of the best songs on it, according to Baz. The song suffers a bit from overproduction, lots of sound effects and various bleeps and noises, but there is a very strong chorus. The arrangement was kicked about a bit, and apparently, Paul wasn't too happy about it, wanting it the way he'd written it. JJ and Dave worked on the middle eight for quite a while to get it super tight, and Baz and Paul worked closely to get the vocal harmonies right. Paul told me in 2023 that the song is an anti-war song, in particular, anti-Gulf War and anti-Bush.

Contemporary Tracks

'Life's Too Short'

The B-side to 'Long Black Veil'. A bit of a lost Stranglers classic, written and sung by JJ, it was the first song that Baz recorded with the band. The band worked hard on it altogether in the little studio they were using at the time and pieced it together bit by bit to make all the sections work and join up perfectly. There are some nice musical touches on this, particularly the vibes, which I suspect were keyboard-produced.

JJ's lyrics are about making the most of the time you have to the fullest as he outlines a trip he made with his partner on a bike: 'RS Sprint to Portsmouth'. An RS Sprint is a Triumph motorcycle and it's still the same one he has to this day.

Suite XVI (2006)

Personnel:
Jean-Jacques Burnel: bass guitar, vocals
Baz Warne: guitar, vocals, harmonica, Jew's Harp
Dave Greenfield: keyboards, vocals
Jet Black: drums, percussion
Additional personnel:
Paul Roberts: percussion (on 'Anything Can Happen')
Lucy Lewry: backing vocals (on 'Bless You (Save You, Spare You, Damn You'))
Recorded at Charlton Farm Studios, Bath, in 2006
Producer: Louie Nicastro
Executive Producers: The Stranglers and Sil Willcox
Engineer: Louie Nicastro
Original UK label and catalogue number: Liberty/EMI Records 0946 371386 2 5
Released: 18 September 2006 (UK)
Highest chart position: UK: 89 (although the Official Charts Company has it at number 45 in the UK, number seven in the Scottish Album Chart and number four in the UK Independent Album Chart)
Running time: 40.27
All tracks written by The Stranglers (Jean-Jacques Burnel, Baz Warne, Dave Greenfield, Jet Black), except 'Unbroken' (Black, Burnel, Greenfield, Roberts, Warne), 'See Me Coming' (Burnel)

The Stranglers were on the climb having released *Norfolk Coast*, a critically successful album and one that was seemingly a return to form. They needed to build on that, and the management company had arranged for a house to be rented in Looe in Cornwall for the band to work in. JJ and Baz went down there together in January 2005 to start the process and got a lot done. They were writing for hours every day and night, too. A total of about 30 songs were written. However, this upset Paul a great deal as he hadn't been invited.

The cracks were starting to appear. For starters, when the band started collating material for the next record, they all tossed their ideas in and arranged some time together to start sifting and rejecting at their HQ in Somerset. There were tensions in the house and Paul wouldn't stay, electing instead to drive the 180-mile round trip every day from the south coast, where he was then living, a practice he'd started during the *Norfolk Coast* sessions, which were now an accepted part of his routine. There appeared to be a wall going up between the singer and the rest of the band. This, along with the fact that he wasn't invited to Looe along with JJ and Baz, led to some tensions. According to Baz, 'it was becoming more difficult to all be in the same room together for the necessary time to work on all the stuff we had ... it was fucking frustrating, to say the least'.

Then, one day, there was a padded envelope on the doormat in Looe with some songs from Paul on a CD, but due to the tensions between him and JJ in particular at the time, it was never opened while they were there. When it was eventually opened and played, the band already had most of what they needed. Baz Warne takes up the story:

> Things came to a head when he turned up to record one day having not bothered to learn the words to the song we were doing ['A Soldier's Diary'], which was unusual for him as he was usually the consummate pro, always giving it 100% with whatever we were involved in, and never settled for anything second best … even during the most stressful times. It was the beginning of the end. The producer complained, a meeting was called and Paul quit. He was given some time to think it over and make a choice … go on the road for the next four months with an album he felt he had no real part of, with a band he was becoming increasingly distant from and with a crew who didn't want to work with him any more … or leave for pastures new with a clean break and blank canvas. I think anyone would have done what he did next in that situation, to be honest. He'd completed about two-thirds of the record, and there are versions of the finished songs with his voice on them and some typically good Paul vocals, but he'd just had enough … and to those ends, so had everyone else … 16 years and he was gone.

In 2023, Paul told me:

> I was basically fed up and then pushed. I'd spent 16 years trying to get the band to write – with limited success – then sidelined. I also started to release solo stuff, which one or two people were a bit unhappy with (although I thought that was a thing the band would embrace … until I pursued it!). I think that disillusionment and the need to write more is the best explanation.

Paul's last gig with The Stranglers was at Nottingham's Rock City in December 2005. Apparently, he didn't speak to anyone before, during or after the gig. He left immediately after the show – Hugh-style – but on the way home, he had an accident. Thankfully, he was unhurt, but the car was a write-off.

With a fair amount of tracks for the new album recorded, the band had to decide whether to keep Paul's vocals or erase them and re-record them. They decided to re-record. That meant Baz's first stab at lead vocals and JJ's return to lead vocals after a 16-year break – the band became a quartet again. Baz says: 'We went out and played a show three weeks after we became four again too … and that surpassed all our expectations. It took a while to get used to … but not too long … by the summer of 2006, we had it down … and this album helped start yet another new era for us'.

The album was released on 18 September 2006 with moderate chart success (see above), and one single was taken from it: 'Spectre Of Love'. Many tracks stayed in the live setlist for years, with 'Relentless' still in the set during the 2023 UK tour. The cover is beige, with the band's logo in red and the title (in fancy script) in black, the letter 'S' swirling down to become the tale of the band's rat symbol. Obviously, it's a play on words – 'Sweet 16' becomes *Suite XIV* – this being the band's 16th studio album. Why the Black Widow spider is there is anybody's guess.

'Unbroken'

The first song from the album was brought in by JJ, who had most of the chorus and some parts of the verses written. Once he played the bass line, Baz thought of adding a guitar similar in style to Nirvana – raw and dirty, as the song is a bit of a rocker. There is light and shade in the music and lyrics, which are autobiographical, especially when he sings about being 'beaten nearly dead' (some of the early-days shenanigans, no doubt). JJ sings the verses and Baz the choruses, as he says, 'somehow it seemed more amusing to have a big shaven-headed northerner singing about wearing suspenders. To this day, I'm not sure if that line was thrown in for effect or whether JJ has actually done it. He hasn't said ... but knowing him...' Actually, JJ has dragged up in the past: on the cover of *10,* for instance, and with Dave for the *Fire And Water* album they did together.

'Spectre Of Love'

A song by Baz about the turmoil he was feeling regarding his daughter's refusal to speak to him. She was a teenager at the time and didn't speak to her dad for five years. This song was written two years into that period. The words, 'I should have wrapped you up and kept you safe/Instead I turned my back on you', denotes Baz's regret about this time. Baz affirms that music should remind people of both good and bad times, and the band knew what this song meant to Baz and put in a great performance.

The band, yet again, match dark subject matter with upbeat music; even the chorus is a bit 'singalong'. The song flows along thanks to a great synthesiser line and the superb riff by JJ and Baz just before the second verse. Baz remembers: 'We played it live very early on and it was heart-warming to see the crowd singing along with every word from the start. There were a few reservations about a Stranglers song with the word 'love' in the title, but I was adamant it should stay, and I'm pleased it did'.

'Spectre Of Love' was the only single released from the album on 11 September 2006 on Liberty Records (3750 357). The CD single had a live version of 'Instead Of This' as an extra track, and the bright-green vinyl version had a live version of 'Death And Night And Blood' on the flip side. The single reached number 57 in the UK charts and the live tracks were recorded at The Shepherd's Bush Empire in London on 2 December 2005.

'She's Slipping Away'

'She's Slipping Away' was one of the songs that the departed Paul Roberts had a hand in. He wrote the lyrics with Baz (who sings) after the latter had read a newspaper report about a man who knocked his girlfriend out and then buried her, thinking he'd killed her. However, she later escaped from the ground and hammered on a neighbour's door for help.

There is the 'light and dark' juxtaposition between the chorus and verse, but the band didn't want to distract people from the story. However, just before the guitar solo, the producer gives it a bit of a demonic twist by detuning Baz's voice on the word 'soul'. You can also hear Baz laughing into the guitar's pick-up during the solo. Baz had a little Gibson Melody Maker guitar, which, at some time, had the pickup taken out of it and put back in the wrong way round, giving it a slightly microphonic tone at times. It made for a good effect.

'Summat Outanowt'

Meaning 'Something out of Nothing' in a northern/Yorkshire/Lancashire type accent, this was one of the first songs JJ and Baz had written in Cornwall the previous year. The core bass line and guitar hook came from a jam session one night, and the next day, JJ had most of the lyrics, which detail a relationship he'd had with a girl in his youth who made mountains out of molehills ('you blow hot and cold'), blowing everything out of all proportion. The 'bad albino' line is a reference to the character of Silas in the movie *The Da Vinci Code*, and the 'rabbit horror show' is a reference to the movie *Fatal Attraction* and the 'bunny boiler' (Glenn Close).

JJ sat with his bass for hours working out the bass solo in the middle, honing it and streamlining it, then Baz joined in at the end on guitar and that was the whole middle eight. This was the first song to be recorded for the album, and according to Baz, there's an amusing outtake of Paul venting his spleen. He either couldn't get the words right or was showing his frustration at somebody. Strangely, JJ sings this one when it might have been more appropriate, with it being a northern phrase for the title, for Baz to have sung it. Having said that, this is the closest song to the 1970s Stranglers you can get.

'Anything Can Happen'

This song, written and sung by JJ, is the only track on the album where we can still hear Paul Roberts – but on percussion, not singing. It started life as a medium-paced rocker, but the band got bored and it got shelved for a while. During the original recording sessions with Paul Roberts, there was a huge argument. Paul just wasn't delivering it the way JJ wanted. Paul would always put his own spin on the lyrics and mould them to himself, which is what you'd expect from a singer, but the cracks in the band were widening by this time and the pair of them were goading each other – it just blew right up. According to Baz, they were 'Two crimson-faced blokes right in each other's faces. The day's work was over and me and Dave went to the pub and Jet went home. Dunno what the other two did, but neither of them was there when we got back'. As a result, this was one of the last songs to be recorded. By the time the band looked at it again, they were a four-piece, and they gave it a total overhaul. JJ's lyrics are about George W. Bush and the then-ongoing war in the Middle East, and it suited the more mellow approach. Baz worked out just one guitar part with as few overdubs as possible. There's also a great atmospheric solo from Dave, with a counterpoint guitar behind it, which was worked on quite a bit to get right.

'See Me Coming'

JJ had written this track for a Japanese animated version of *The Count Of Monte Cristo* (written by Alexandre Dumas in collaboration with Auguste Maquet) called 'Gankutsuou', which means 'The King Of The Cavern'. The band liked it and appropriated it for the album.

Baz, in particular, was fond of the verses and the turnaround rhythm, where they shout out the name of the lead character in the movie: 'E-D-M-O-N-D'. There are quite a few bleeps and keyboard effects in this, too. This is sung, naturally, by JJ. He had been approached to write the music for the 24-part TV series by the director Mahiro Maeda, who flew to London to ask him in person. JJ and Louie Nicastro played the music and did the arrangements, with additional guitars from Baz and vocals from Phillipa Cookman.

'Bless You (Save You, Spare You, Damn You)'

Baz wrote the lyrics for this one and he collaborated with JJ for the music. The idea came from a discussion about nursery rhymes, and 'Ring A Ring A Roses' especially. It is thought that the rhyme is connected to the Great Plague of 1664-6 and another saying from that time: 'Bless You (you've sneezed once), Save you (twice), Spare You (thrice) and Damn You' (you've sneezed four times ... you're dead). Baz thought it was a great idea for a song and very quickly wrote the lyrics.

Baz thought the idea of an old rock 'n' roll song-style intro was a good one and came up with the chords. When it came to the first chorus, he thought some female vocals would be great. During Baz and JJ's time in Cornwall the previous year, one of the girls in the estate agents, where they'd rented the house, turned out to be very musical and had a fantastic voice. Her name is Lucy Lewry. JJ and Baz went down to the local pub (The Bullers in Looe) one night for an open mic night and heard her sing. They called her and she did a great job of making the chorus haunting and very atmospheric.

The middle eight is superb. JJ came up with a great chord sequence, which is basically the intro chords in double time. Then, Dave worked out the fantastic Elizabethan-style baroque melody and underpinning it all is some brushwork by Jet. Then, the full band play the whole middle section again and it gets a bit bluesy at the end.

'A Soldier's Diary'

The fastest song the band has ever recorded. They wanted to cram in as many chord changes as they could and still keep the whole thing rocketing along. It was inspired by reading about some of the notes, letters and diaries that were found in the Allied trenches during the First World War, left by soldiers about to go over the top, never to be seen, and in many cases, never to be found again. Baz was really moved by it and put the song together. Counterpointing dark subject matter again with a jolly upbeat tune and melody seems to be key here, and the band rattled this off in no time once they'd worked it through.

'Barbara (Shangri-La)'

Our first love stays in our minds and this Baz song is about his first girlfriend when he was 15 years old. Apparently, she wore a particular perfume, which he remembered well. To be honest, they do say that smells trigger memories better than anything else, and this would seem to be proven by this song. He was sorting some boxes out in his attic and found a perfume tester; the perfume was Barbara's and the memories came flooding back. JJ suggested that he write a song about it and this is the result.

The band tried many arrangements and titles before they were satisfied. Baz plays a 12-string Rickenbacker guitar and Dave supplies synthesised theremin to give it a 'Good Vibrations' feel. The band had sourced a real theremin, but due to it being a difficult instrument to manage, they used a synthesiser.

To this day, Baz still wonders if Barbara has heard this song.

'I Hate You'

When JJ played this song to Baz, he fell about laughing and told him the band should use it. Baz had just gotten hold of a Fender Stratocaster, which is not a model of guitar he has too much love for, but he thought it would be great on this as a kind of Johnny Cash pastiche. Jet's brushwork on this is superb and he really kicks it along in the up-tempo sections. Baz plays harmonica and JJ's vocal and bass lines are exemplary. There was a Jew's, or jaw harp (or juice harp, or mouth harp) lying around, and for a laugh, Baz started playing it under the harmonica solo, never thinking it would be used. The next day, Baz says, 'there it was in the mix'. There's even a phone call there, too. For years, there have been debates regarding the identity of the individual in the song. In 2023, JJ told me that it was about Hugh Cornwell.

'Relentless'

'Relentless' was the last song to be recorded and is a superb finale to the album. In the years since it was recorded, it has become both a fan's and a band favourite. Dave Greenfield, before he died, rated it as one of his top three band songs.

In a discussion between producer Louie Nicastro and Baz, Louie said that the band needed a song that 'hammers along ... something relentless'. Baz then thought, rather than making the actual music relentless, write about things that just never stop: time and tide, love, all things that are eternal. Baz says:

> The lyrics [which he sings] came pretty quickly, but I laboured long and hard to try and find the right guitar riff … it sounds simple on the record, and it is, but therein lies its power. It took a day of just playing it over and over until I found it … the test is always playing it to the band, and once they got their hands on it, it came to life … I knew it would make sense, but everyone working on it shifts it, and it pulls and pushes and moulds itself into the finished article.

Dave's keyboards and JJ's driving bass just drive the song relentlessly.

Giants (2012)

Personnel:
Jean-Jacques Burnel: bass guitar, vocals
Baz Warne: guitar, vocals
Dave Greenfield: keyboards, vocals
Jet Black: drums, percussion
Additional personnel:
Neil Sparkes: additional percussion (on 'My Fickle Resolve' and 'Time Was Once On My Side')
Recorded at Charlton Farm Studios, Bath, between 2011 and 2012
Producer: Louie Nicastro and The Stranglers
Original UK label and catalogue number: Coursegood CG005, Absolute (UK), Ear Music (Europe)
Released: 5 March 2012 (UK)
Highest chart position: UK: 48, France: 121
Running time: 43.07
All tracks written by The Stranglers (Jean-Jacques Burnel, Baz Warne, Dave Greenfield, Jet Black)

There was a five-and-a-half-year wait for the next album, but when it came, it was a cracker! Some of the tracks had been written for the *Suite XIV* album but hadn't made the final cut, and again, it was JJ and Baz who wrote most of the songs. With the band now a four-piece, it was decided, like with the previous album, that lead vocals would be shared between the two writers. Therefore, Baz sang lead on five tracks and JJ on three; they shared one and another was an instrumental.

During the wait, we'd had the career-defining compilation *Decades Apart*, which saw the light of day in 2010. It contained two brand-new tracks: 'Retro Rockets' and 'I Don't See The World Like You Do'. 'Retro Rockets' was released as a download-only single (see 'Assorted Compilations' section).

Giants would be the last album to feature drummer Jet Black, who had been suffering from ill health since 2007. Always a corpulent man, Jet began to suffer heart problems, which led to him missing some gigs. For these, drum technician Ian Barnard and occasionally Neil Sparkes would step in. Jet ceased touring abroad in 2007 but still played in the UK tours, although he missed a few dates in 2008. After falling ill again in 2012, he began to cut down on his appearances. He would still go on tour with them and sign stuff at gigs but only played half a gig, with new drummer Jim Macauley playing the rest. However, they could only do this where there was room on stage for a second drum kit (more about Jet in the next chapter).

Giants continued where *Suite XIV* left off, building on their mix of contemporary sounds with The Stranglers of the 1970s. The album was released on CD, vinyl and digital download. Also, there was the 'deluxe' version, which had a second disc – a 14-track live acoustic set recorded at

The Stranglers' Convention in 2011, featuring the Burnel, Warne, Greenfield, Black line-up.

The album cover caused controversy, as David Boni's image showed (apart from the red band logo and title in white) a children's playground swing, with the four band members hanging by their necks from the frame while a schoolgirl looks up at them. It was deemed a little too much for some countries where the image was banned. In these territories, and for the official promotional disc, the image was the same, except for the fact that the nooses were empty. Another promotional image used in the album lyric booklet showed the four band members dead, with the nooses around their necks. This image was partially banned from the London Underground digital billboards, only being allowed to be shown between 21.00 and 05.00. Rather tellingly, a band portrait used on the actual CD and the inside of the 'deluxe' version has Jet Black with an oxygen mask!

The band undertook a lengthy tour to promote the album and it scraped into the top 50 album chart in the UK at number 48. It also returned them to the French charts at number 121.

'Another Camden Afternoon'

This was originally inspired by an article JJ read about a mugging that took place in Camden, where the assailants ran down a woman in their car to get her bag. After writing the song, JJ and Baz decided to leave out the lyrics as they weren't happy with them, and it became one of the rare Stranglers instrumentals – apart from the backing vocals. The guitar is the dominant instrument here, setting the scene with a very eerie opening – it could almost be a film theme. I wonder if we'll ever get to hear the version with the lyrics at some point.

'Freedom Is Insane'

This track was left over from the songwriting session in Looe, which provided the songs to *Suite XIV*. Baz remembers coming down one morning to find that JJ had been up for hours staring at the sea and writing the lyrics to this one. JJ also sings on it and puts in a great vocal performance. Baz had the ideas for the music. The track was also a live favourite and was in the set for a few years until it made way for tracks off *Dark Matters*. The sound of the sea introduces the track with some delicate keyboard and guitar before launching into a rockier, more up-tempo piece. Two-thirds of the way through, we get a Dave Greenfield keyboard solo. The lyrics evoke emotions about the sea as the singer witnesses its beauty: 'Early morning my eyes gaze across the sea/ no-one has ever walked here except you and me'.

'Giants'

This is a song about the captains of industry and how the world we live in today was shaped, as well as its pitfalls. The line, 'I'm glad my father's not here to see what happened to men like him', says it all. With JJ singing the verses and Baz the choruses, we're treated to a double vocal onslaught. This was a joint composition between the two frontmen. The mix of the synthesiser and menacing guitar is the highlight of this mid-tempo song.

'Lowlands'

I'll let Baz tell the story of 'Lowlands':

> This was inspired by the first acoustic tour we did with Neil Sparkes in Holland and Belgium in 2007 and one mad night in particular when we were driving back from a gig to the hotel we were using as a base. We had plenty of brandy and primo Dutch weed and started to record ourselves a cappella, making up a song. Dave was in the front singing the keyboard parts, I was singing bass parts, JJ was singing the melody and Sparkes was keeping time on a champagne bottle with a broken drumstick. Our tour manager Gary Knighton was laughing so much he could hardly drive and was getting secondarily stoned.

The version as recorded on the album is sung by Baz, and he and JJ put the lyrics together. Basically, it tells the story of life on the road.

'Boom Boom'

A different feel from anything the band have done before greets us in the form of a 'choppy' Rolling Stones-like rhythm with a jangle and a bit of swagger. Sung by Baz, who wrote the lyrics, unsurprisingly, this is about a girl (well, there's a surprise) and the fact that, sometimes, the singer doesn't fancy her. Musically, this is a group effort, with the whole band chipping in. Another example of a downbeat lyric teamed with an upbeat melody.

'My Fickle Resolve'

'My Fickle Resolve' has a laid-back feel, aided by some lovely brushwork from Jet and Dave's 'trippy', psychedelic sound, similar to the keyboards on 'European Female'; he also plays a wonderful solo at the end. JJ plays acoustic bass. As with most of the album, the band tried to keep it as stripped back as possible. Like 'Boom Boom', Baz supplied the lyrics and vocals and was composed by the band. Baz almost speaks the lyrics for the most part as he bemoans his inability to fathom women out. However, he is determined to do it, even though 'my fickle resolve will be/the death of me I'm sure'.

'Time Was Once On My Side'

A song that just moves and grooves in a pleasant manner, this is really upbeat. JJ came up with the lyrics, which he also sings (with some saturation), and originally sang the words down the phone to Baz when he first wrote them. Neil Sparkes provides some tremendous conga work, especially at the end, making this a proper 'feel good' song. This is about a man who has 'screwed up' one relationship, but 'I was handed a second chance/from the gods of true romance'. However, he's not getting any younger; he has to do it now as 'Time was once on my side', but it might not be now. As mentioned earlier, the band generally work together on the music, this creates the 'Stranglers sound', and this is a prime example of that, with the rhythmic bass, pounding rhythm, rock guitar and Dave's keyboards holding it all together.

'Mercury Rising'

This song has the feel of The Stranglers' mid-80s period, with a slightly more polished production indicative of the era, and a lovely, swirling keyboard riff. JJ provides a melodic bass line in line with the keyboards, which keeps the whole thing together, and Baz does his best Captain Beefheart impression on the vocals (almost chanted) and slide guitar. At first, the protagonist was down, but then 'the atmosphere began to crackle and fizz' and the mercury (in his personal barometer) began to rise.

This was the sole single from the album, released on 29 October 2012 on Absolute Records (CG006). Released as a CD single, the main track was included in an edited form, along with live versions of 'Sometimes' and 'Mercury Rising', recorded during the *Giants* tour, and an instrumental version of 'Mercury Rising'. Sadly, it didn't chart anywhere.

'Adios (Tango)'

This a heavy metal tango sung in Spanish, according to Baz. It has a great intro, with a rhythmic keyboard and fuzz guitar. With it being sung in a foreign language (apart from the last three lines), and since the song was his idea, it's JJ singing about saying 'goodbye'. Luckily, the lyrics in the CD booklet are in English.

'15 Steps'

The band spent almost three years at their base in Bath, working on, arranging and sometimes rejecting the songs for the album (and apparently others, as Baz said that there are loads that didn't make it onto the record). It proved to be gruelling and Baz sometimes longed for the sanctuary of his room. He says that, on occasion, when it had been a really hard day, he found himself counting the steps up to his room. Guess what? There were 15: 'There are 15 steps to heaven/Eddie Cochran got it wrong'. This song is about the house and the things that occurred there. For instance, the band used to discuss all manner of things there ('The topics include dust, to the state of the nation') and it was apparently meant to be haunted ('Late at night you might hear voices'). Baz gives his all on this great finale to the album. The tempo barrels along at a great pace, and overall, it is quite a good rocker.

Dark Matters (2021)

Personnel:
Jean-Jacques Burnel: bass guitar, vocals, acoustic guitar (on 'The Lines')
Baz Warne: guitar, vocals
Dave Greenfield: keyboards, vocals
Jim Macaulay: drums, percussion, vocals
Additional personnel:
Louie Nicastro: additional keyboards
Matthew Bourne-Jones: trumpet (on 'If Something's Gonna Kill Me (It Might As Well Be Love)')
Recorded at Charlton Farm Studios, Bath, OX4 Sound Studios, Oxford, Baz Warne home studio, Yorkshire. Unknown studio, France, between 2019 and 2021
Producer: Louie Nicastro
Executive Producers: The Stranglers and Sil Willcox
Original UK label and catalogue number: Coursegood CGCD12
Released: 10 September 2021 (UK)
Highest chart position: UK: 4, Belgium: 152
Running time: 42.55
All tracks written by The Stranglers (Jean-Jacques Burnel, Baz Warne, Dave Greenfield, Jim Macaulay), except 'This Song' written by Mathew Seamarks and The Stranglers

In the nine years between *Giants* and *Dark Matters*, lots of things happened, both in the world of The Stranglers and the world in general, and all of this contributed to what JJ has called 'the best album we've done'. The band were now approaching their 40th anniversary. In fact, on the 2013 tour, Dave's keyboards had a sign on stating 'Almost There'. And the year after, they did get there. JJ posted a message on the band's website, which read: 'On this, the occasion of our Ruby Anniversary, I would like to take this opportunity to stick my fingers up to everyone who wrote us off and dismissed us'. Then, he added, 'However, I would like to thank those who saw beyond the words of the critics and drew their own conclusions'. I was lucky enough to interview Jet Black in the lead-up to the 40th Anniversary tour – *The Ruby Tour* – and he attributed the band's longevity to a growth in maturity: 'Over the years, we have all become more professional and we take the business of music more seriously'.

In the absence of new music, the band's management released three live albums on their Coursegood label: *Feel It Live* (2013), *Black And White Live* (2016) and *Rattus Relived* (2017).

By this time, Jet had retired from playing live due to his worsening health. For a while, he hadn't played abroad and his participation in UK gigs was limited. For instance, during *The Ruby Tour* at the Manchester show on 29 March 2014, he only played four songs: three during the main show and 'Tank' during the encore. The rest of the drumming was done by new recruit Jim Macaulay. Jet's last performance with the band was at the

Cambridge Corn Exchange on 20 March 2015. Jim, born on 13 April 1984 in Birmingham, first met the band in 2011 while he was drumming for Mike Marlin, who was one of the support bands on the 2011 UK tour. At that time, when Jet was unable to play, Ian Barnard was filling in; however, the next year, Ian was offered work elsewhere and was unable to cover for Jet in the Festivals. So, Ian asked Jim to cover for him. When he was offered more work, Ian never returned and Jim carried on. He says, 'I never actually got asked to join the band, but there's a lot of songs to learn, so getting someone better would be a right pain in the arse for them at this stage. I'm also the only one who knows how to plug all the gear in'. Jet remained involved with the band but eventually retired in 2018. He sadly died at his Welsh home on 6 December 2022 at the age of 84. Before he died, however, he heard the new album and gave it the 'thumbs up'.

The band, with Jim, went into the studio to start work on a new album and had quite a lot of work completed when... COVID happened. The Stranglers had just returned from a tour of Australia and New Zealand, the last gig being at the Auckland Town Hall, New Zealand, on 15 February 2020. The UK then went into lockdown a month later. Dave was in hospital having treatment for heart-related problems. On 29 April, he was diagnosed with COVID-19 and died a week later on 3 May 2020. JJ, in lockdown in the south of France, was bereft; Baz, at home in Yorkshire, was so upset that he turned his phone off completely for a week. Eventually, after about a month, they realised that there were some difficult decisions to make. Do they carry on? Or do they call it a day? A tour was booked but obviously postponed due to the pandemic; the band were unsure if honouring these dates once the lockdown was lifted was suitable. In the end, after speaking to Dave's widow Pam, they decided to carry on. Baz says:

> We decided the first priority would be to finish the recordings we'd started with Dave and honour his memory. Once we started to revisit the rough tracks we had, it was very painful to hear him playing so well and even his voice on talk back from time to time talking to the engineer ... very difficult. But it also seemed to open up a seam of creativity, particularly in JJ, who was very isolated down in the south of France. He just got his guitar out, put pen to paper and wrote a lot ... the most he'd written in years ... some of it fantastic. For my part, I had my studio here in Yorkshire and was only too happy to spend 12-hour days sitting at my computer writing and recording. JJ would send me what he had and just say, 'do what you like', with most of it. He had some specific ideas, too, and as we've worked together for over two decades, we have a very easy and understanding partnership when it comes to writing songs, and we were able to communicate our ideas to each other smoothly and easily ... we got through it. At one point, we were calling each other half a dozen times a day and ideas were whizzing through the ether at an alarming rate. I was sending stems and ideas to Louie [Nicastro] down in

> Bath, and slowly but surely, it all started to come together. Sitting listening to the final mixes in order two years later was a very sobering experience, and I'd be lying if I said we didn't raise a glass or two ... both to ourselves and our fallen comrade, even before *Dark Matters* came out, just because ... well, we'd done it. It didn't matter to us whether it was a success or not, although you'd like that, of course ... but we didn't give a toss ... we just wanted to make it for Dave so that the world could hear his final contributions to his remarkable career ... and for his wife Pam, who'd given us her blessing to just 'get it out there' ... there were tears shed from all of us.

Of course, they had to pay tribute to Dave, and three more songs were recorded: 'And If You Should See Dave…', 'If Something's Gonna Kill Me' and 'Down'. Not only were they without their keyboard player, but this was also the first album not to feature Jet Black. Jim Macaulay stepped up to the mark.

Dark Matters was released on 10 September 2021 and was preceded by the digital-only release of 'And If You Should See Dave…' in May and 'If Something's Gonna Kill Me' in August. 'This Song' was released on the same day as the album. Much of the album is a change of pace for the band; they are more mature now and are more comfortable with the slower and reflective songs. It was a great success, reaching number four on the charts. 'These days, the charts don't mean so much to us', stated JJ in an interview with this author. 'However, it gives us some bragging rights and is a "finger up" to those who said that we couldn't do anything fresh. It proves that there's no age limit to musical ability. We are all delighted with the album. It's about the world we're living in'.

The cover shows four of the Easter Island Moai, the monolithic human figures that were carved by the Rapa Pui people between 1250 and 1500 AD. Whether these figures were meant to represent the four Stranglers is open to conjecture.

Those who pre-ordered the album were given a bonus CD – *Dave Greenfield – A Tribute* – featuring eight tracks, four of which starred Dave as lead singer; two were early live recordings of tracks from *Dark Matters* (see 'Live Recordings').

'Water'

'Water' had its origins in the *Giants* sessions. The Stranglers have never thrown ideas away, and when they start work on a new album, they sift through old demos to see if there is anything worth salvaging. Baz had become, very early on, the custodian of the material the band were amassing, as he told me in 2023:

> It's a role I'd fallen into right from the early days of my time in the group when we lived at Charlton Farm in Somerset for eight months, getting songs together for what would become *Norfolk Coast*. I enjoyed getting up early and listening back to what we'd done the night before, deleting the crap and

> keeping ideas to play to JJ and Dave when we started work again later in the day. It sort of became my 'job' and I became very possessive of it.

He was going through some old tapes and came across this track. JJ wrote the lyrics and the two of them put the music together and recorded a demo. They put a lot of work into it, recording guitar and bass, backing vocals and solos, but strangely forgot about it. Baz sent the demo to JJ, who said it was great. It was polished up and rearranged and Dave and Jim added the keyboards and drums. It was the first song from the new album that the band played live, and they started road-testing it a year before it was eventually recorded.

The atmospheric intro with echo-y guitar slowly builds into a mid-tempo rocker. A very strong bass line runs through the whole song, and the keyboards from Dave were put together after he had heard the original demo, which had no keyboards on it at all.

This was JJ's tirade about the Arab Spring, which was a series of anti-government protests, that took place in the Arab world from 2010 onwards about corruption and the poor economies in that part of the world. From 2010, it spread westwards and south and eventually led to reforms in most countries and the ousting of Presidents in at least four countries. Approximately 61,000 people were killed in the protests ('The crescent moon was aflame/innocent people were slain') and JJ makes the analogy that water is synonymous with freedom and democracy. He also wanted to make a big statement and, therefore, wanted the track to sound big – like a 'stadium' song.

'This Song'

The origins of this came from a band called Disciples of Spess, who recorded some songs with producer Louie Nicastro. One of the songs, written by band member Matthew Seamarks, was called 'This Song Will Get Me Over You'. Nicastro thought it might be a good song to 'stranglerise'. The band, who tend to very rarely only cover established artists, were reluctant at first, but Seamarks gave the band carte blanche and they rearranged it, changed some words and added more keyboards (receiving a co-writer credit) – it became a live favourite.

It was released as the third and last single from the album on 10 September 2021 as a digital download, but sadly, it didn't chart, despite a video starring Stuart 'Psycho' Pearce, ex-footballer and old friend and fan of the band.

Sung by Baz, it tells of someone who is trying to get over pain and heartbreak by putting their memories and feelings for the person in a box and burying them at sea. He then uses the power of music to get over the pain.

'And If You Should See Dave...'

Since this was a very personal song to the band, I'll let Baz tell the story:

> One obvious huge hole in the band was our beloved keyboard player. His passing was a massive shock to us all and it threatened to end the band

> there and then. We really couldn't see how we'd be able to continue without him, and everything went on hold indefinitely. JJ wrote the lyrics to this and had all the parts, too, although the song needed a proper arrangement. He sent me what he had [he'd demoed it on his phone] and I set to work on it. We decided pretty much from the outset that this song wouldn't have any keyboards on it at all, and so it remains, to the best of my knowledge, the only Stranglers song ever to have none at all [the absence of keyboards speaks volumes]. The guitars and backing vocals were all done at my house and I arranged it the way you hear it today. JJ sings this beautifully [Baz sings the bridge] and it's a very heartfelt tribute to his mate. They'd been together for 45 years ... I'd been with Dave for 20 and it killed me that he'd gone ... God knows what it was like for JJ after over twice as long. The two of us do a stripped-down version live with just two guitars sometimes, and you can hear a pin drop when we play it ... usually.

The last two lines are very poignant: 'It would be nice to say hello/This is where your solo would go'.

This was the first single to be released from the album – as a digital download – on 14 May 2021, but it didn't trouble the chart compilers. The video is worth watching as there are many visual references to their fallen comrade.

'If Something's Gonna Kill Me (It Might As Well Be Love)'

This is another tribute to Dave, again written by JJ and arranged by Baz and Louie Nicastro. The band have their own group chat so they can all keep in touch with each other wherever they are in the world. One day, again during lockdown, JJ just sent this title to the rest of the band as a suggestion for a song. He was the first in the band to come up with an idea for the song, which is what was recorded. It was literally him and an acoustic guitar. Baz immediately thought that they could do some kind of electro-pop treatment with it, similar to Kraftwerk – it took him a day to arrange. All the guitars you hear on the finished album version were kept from Baz's demo, and Louie replaced all the keyboards, drums and bass synthesiser parts. Usually, in The Stranglers, but not always, the person responsible for writing the lyrics and top-line melody sings the track – not so with this one. Baz sang on the demo, but obviously, JJ wanted to sing the final thing himself. There then followed (according to Baz) a fairly good-natured power struggle over who should sing it. JJ went off to some studio near his house and did a version, but by his own admission, Baz's voice was more suited to it, so he redid the vocal in the studio with Louie, and that's the one you hear. JJ wrote the song, but because the drums and bass are synths, and Louie redid all the keyboards, Baz is the only Strangler appearing to appear on this song. The synthesisers are the ones that Dave used – Oberheim and Mini Moog. Special mention should go to Matt Bourne-Jones, who plays sublime trumpet on this track and, in particular, a beautiful jazzy, freeform solo.

The lines, 'You wake up one morning and the world has changed' and 'our ranks are getting thinner by the day', say it all, really.

This was the second single from the album, released as a digital download on 7 August 2021. It didn't chart.

'No Man's Land'

Drummer Jim Macaulay wrote the lyrics and most of the music for this. Baz sings it. Jim says:

> The song was written during lockdown. I got a job as a delivery driver and I was just spending all day driving around listening to the news and gradually becoming more and more convinced that our glorious leaders had no idea what they were up to. Specifically, it's about Dominic Cummings and his trip to Barnard Castle (his infamous drive to the castle so that he could 'check his eyesight'), just the overwhelming arrogance of thinking the people you were elected to serve are just sheep who'll believe any old bullshit you feed them.

He continues, 'I contributed to several of the songs on *Dark Matters* – obviously drum and rhythm parts, but also arrangements and things when we were still all doing it in a room together pre-pandemic. I really enjoy writing as a band in a room. I think it yields the most interesting results'.

The verses are quite jerky (you definitely couldn't dance to it), and the chant at the end – 'Nobody move nobody gets hurt...' – is quite venomous.

'The Lines'

JJ came up with the original idea, the melody and most of the lyrics, then one night, over a bottle (or two) of wine, he and Baz finished it off. They went into the studio the next day to record it before they forgot what they had worked out, and it was done in one take. JJ plays acoustic guitar and Baz sings. They spent a long time thinking about whether they should add keyboards; by the time they opted for it, Dave had passed, so Louie Nicastro added the organ.

The emotive lyrics tell of looking in the mirror and seeing the lines on your face as you get older and what causes them – your parents, children, drinking, smoking, frowns and laughter. As JJ was approaching his 70th birthday, this was him addressing his older self.

'Payday'

Another JJ lyric with music by JJ and Baz, but instead of JJ, it's a Baz vocal. This is probably because of the complex bassline, which would have made it a little problematic in a live setting, especially as it was performed heavily on the 2019 UK tour. To be honest, JJ later admitted that Baz sang it better than he did. The backing track was recorded almost immediately after the band came off the road so that it was still fresh in their minds, but they worked on it for quite some time.

'Payday' is about comeuppance and that you sometimes reap what you sew. For instance, the philosopher Socrates was sentenced to death for impiety and corruption of the young. He drank the poison hemlock. The reference to Alexander the Great stems from the fact that when he died, his generals carved up his empire, and, of course, this led to Ptolemy and Cleopatra in Egypt.

Baz remembers: 'Some great piano from Dave on this one. I also have a vivid recollection of him and I sitting in a studio somewhere late one night working out the solo sections to this...we were fairly 'merry' if memory serves'. Baz also gets tongue-tied when, instead of singing 'bitter and twisted', he sings 'Bisted and Twitter'. The band liked it so much that they kept it in, and it almost became the title of the album.

'Down'

'Down' is JJ's love song to his other half and the lyrics are very heartfelt. He recorded the vocals quickly to capture the initial moment of emotion. There are some wavers and tiny timing issues, but it's honest, and that's what he wanted. As Baz explains, 'it doesn't always have to be technically on the money ... you can lose beauty in the pursuit of perfection a lot of the time'. Baz came up with the riff for the acoustic guitar on the spot – a piece of technical expertise. The electric guitar that sounds like a lap steel is actually a backwards patch on a fairly old bit of guitar technology called a Pod. Mr Warne was messing about in the living room of the house that the band were living in. He tried the backward patch that his guitar had, and JJ came dashing in shouting, 'that's it!' The gentle, strummed chords are very effective. Louie added the beautiful piano part and that was enough. Anything else would have spoiled it.

'The Last Men On The Moon'

Another classic example of the band not throwing anything away. Baz had this song mostly formed for the best part of ten years, composed using a Burns baritone guitar. He takes up the story:

> I'd played it to JJ a couple of times over the years and he liked it, then he didn't, depending on what sort of mood he was in. One day, I finally sat him down and wouldn't let him out of the room until he'd given it his full, undivided attention. He sort of looked at me and went, 'what a great song ... why haven't you played me this before?' What can you say?

This was another song that was thoroughly road-tested on the 2019 tour; it went down a storm and fans were asking if it had been recorded. The whole band contributed to the music when recording the song. JJ plays a clever stuttering sort of bassline and ventures up the neck a lot so as not to get in the way of the baritone guitar. It sounds very deep and isn't that far away from the bass guitar in terms of frequency. Baz tuned his guitar to A instead of B, where most baritones are, and it gives it a real growl. Dave's soaring keyboard riff is pure Greenfield, and apparently, he loved to play this.

The lyrics came from a comment by Mrs Warne about the Russians firing geckos up into space, so Baz ran with the idea whilst addressing the issue of junk floating around up there. Baz also has his voice processed at the end of the song to give it a more futuristic, robotic sound.

'White Stallion'

JJ wrote the lyrics to this one, which he sang, and he and Baz worked out the music from JJ's acoustic guitar demo. The 'White Stallion' in question is Donald Trump, and the Tiger is China. 'A tiger has been waiting/for his moment to come' alludes to the fact that China's influence on the world is increasing whilst the West's is declining.

Upon hearing JJ play a descending bass line, the idea of a 'disco' feel came to Baz and he recorded a demo and sent it to JJ. 'Fifteen minutes later', says Baz, 'he called me back laughing his arse off ... 'that's brilliant ... let's do it!' Louie Nicastro added the operatic voice breakdown section in the middle using a synthesiser. JJ wanted the song to be 'epic' as it was the last demo session the band did with Dave before COVID hit. They decided to keep the bass line in the verses as a synthesiser to emphasise the 'disco-ness' of it, so JJ plays live bass at the beginning of the track, power chords in the choruses and the part where Baz take over the vocals. Due to COVID, all the guitars were recorded at Baz's home studio.

'Breathe'

The opening riff is something JJ came up with whilst strumming an acoustic guitar, which Baz thought was a winner. Another joint music-arranging session with Baz and JJ resulted in the finished song. For all the power and aggression in JJ's playing that we all know so well, he loves to play fingerstyle, too. The verses are nicely chosen musical phrases, according to Baz – all played with his fingers and not a plectrum – and are very tasteful. There's a beautiful ascending piano riff from Dave in the middle of each chorus, too, which gives the track some real style, and as ever, his playing in this is superb. Sadly, by the time of mixing the album, he'd passed away, so there are some little flourishes from Louie, but most of it is Dave. If JJ could write a song about his 'other half' ('Down'), then Baz Warne could write one about his – and this is it.

Rarities

Throughout the history of any band, there will be some recordings that never properly saw the light of day, and The Stranglers are no exception, but if you look hard enough, they can be found. Many of The Stranglers' 'lost' tracks were released on a CD called *Strangled At Birth,* issued in 1994 by The Stranglers Information Service (SIS CD001), and some of these were released by EMI in 2002 on EMI 7253 5 41079 2.

'Goebbels, Mosley, God And Ingrams'

Originally released by SIS on SIS003 in March 1988 on a flexi-disc, this is a solo JJ Burnel recording from 1980. It was recorded during the sessions for JJ's first solo album at Eden Studios in Chiswick and Spaceward in Cambridge, with engineers Aldo Bocca and Steve Churchyard at the controls. Three songs were demoed, but two of them were never finished as JJ went off on tour. Bass and keyboard-heavy with barely audible vocals, this would have been great if finished.

'Waiting For The Trees To Grow'

This was written and recorded by JJ at the same time as 'Goebbels, Mosley, God And Ingrams'. The third demoed track was 'Girl From The Snow Country', which was almost released as a single in The Netherlands. Like 'Goebbels', this is very experimental and electronic, with JJ saying the title in English, French and German.

'Gone Are Those Days'

This ended up as an unofficial release in Russia as a five-and-a-half-inch flexi-disc. This is nothing more than electronic 'noodling' from JJ that laments times past.

'The Beast'

This is an instrumental outtake from the *Aural Sculpture* sessions recorded in 1984 that features an excellent organ crescendo in the middle. The original version had lyrics about people being attracted to something that is unknown and dangerous. Hugh Cornwell liked it, but JJ wasn't convinced, and the recording was shelved until a few years later when JJ removed the lyrics. The song was later used as the basis for the title track of JJ's solo album *Un Jour Parfait.*

'New Day Today'

Released by SIS (SIS004) in April 1991 as flexi-disc, this lovely piece of music was recorded in 1989 during the sessions for the *10* album. Both Jet and Hugh were not impressed by JJ's vocal delivery, which is rather quiet and in a similar vein to 'La Folie'.

'My Young Dreams'

This was a single released by The Stranglers Information Service (SIS 001) in 1985. The Stranglers had demoed it in Fulham in 1974 and was written by the band (including Hans Warmling and Dave Greenfield). The single was released under the name A Marriage of Convenience and was produced by Jet Black, who also played drums. The vocalist was Chris Twomey, and the B-side was 'Two Sides To Every Story' (on which Jet didn't play). No other Stranglers had a part in either recording.

'Mr Big'

Written by John Ellis, this outtake from *Stranglers In The Night* sessions ended up as an unofficial release in Russia as a five-and-a-half-inch flexi-disc in 1992. According to John Ellis in 2023, this is a stand-alone piece and is not connected to the Mr Big from the track 'Little Blue Lies'. A very sinister bass line underscores this tale of a rich and shady character. However, such wealth could be a fantasy, as suggested in the line, 'the tiny world of Mr Big'. He could be exaggerating his own importance.

'I'll Be Seeing You'

This is another outtake from *Stranglers In The Night* that features a superb vocal from Paul. This is about saying goodbye to someone who has gone out of their life – either through cutting communication or perhaps even through death – but will 'see them everywhere'. Very delicate song, musically.

Other Tracks

'Wasted'

The only recorded version is a 1974 demo recorded in Fulham with original member Hans Warmling. The band had yet to embrace their future image, and this track is a piece of fast-paced seventies pop, with Warmling's electric piano to the fore.

'Mony Mony'

This was recorded by the band and Celia Collin under the name Celia and The Mutations. Released by United Artists in 16977 (UP 36262), it didn't chart. This version is – to be honest – unremarkable, but as a curiosity, very interesting. It has the sound of a band having fun.

'Vladimir And The Pearl'

This is the sixth and final instalment of the Vladimir saga from 1999. Users of the SIS phone service were able to listen to this and later download it via the band's website. Vladimir is now settled in Cuba but has an 'itchy bum' due to eating 'refried beans'. He becomes a pearl fisherman and wants to get to Miami. One day, while out fishing, he finds a big pearl – that's where the Vladimir saga ends. Who wants to write the 'Vladimir' novel?

'Grip '89'

A remixed version of original track released in 1989 on Liberty Records (EM 84). The remix was by Barry Cooder and Taff B Dylan. 'Waltzinblack' was on the B-side. The 12" version had an extra remix and the rare track 'Tomorrow Was The Hereafter'. The track was remixed to promote the compilation album *Singles (The UA Years)*. It reached number 33 in the UK charts.

'Peaches 2004'

'Peaches 2004' was a re-recording. JJ's original bass was sampled for the intro to give it that retro vibe, and as the band took pains to make sure it was the same tempo as the original, it fitted perfectly. However, that was the only bit of the old track that was used. Everything else was re-recorded with Baz Warne on guitars and Paul Roberts' vocal. The track was released as an extra track on CD2 of 'Big Thing Coming'.

'Retro Rockets'

A brand-new song specially recorded for the *Decades Apart* compilation album. Baz wrote it in an afternoon and didn't really think about it again until he played the demo to the band. Both JJ and Dave really liked it and it was recorded. Baz was not keen on how it turned out, as he had, in his words, 'a stinking fucking cold when doing the vocals, and you can really hear it in my voice ... totally bunged up'. The song was performed live and it went down really well. 'Retro Rockets' is basically self-explanatory. There was a short-lived radio programme called 'Retro Rockets' that Baz used to listen to and the music took him back to his youth. Baz says, 'I sort of threw the song off in a couple of hours and have never particularly been keen on it'.

'I Don't See The World Like You Do'

Baz also wrote this song for the *Decades Apart* compilation, which he much preferred and thought should have been the single instead of 'Retro Rockets'. A thudding bass intro delivers a mid-tempo song with a Baz vocal about a couple who both see the world differently.

'(Get A) Grip (On Yourself)' – with Simple Minds

According to Baz Warne, this is probably the rarest Stranglers single. It was recorded at the request of Simple Minds singer Jim Kerr (who was a friend of JJ's), as they had played the song live at gigs and the two bands were due to tour with each other later that year. So, on 9 July 2015 (Jim Kerr's birthday), JJ, Baz and Dave rocked up at Battersea Park Studios with Jim Kerr, Charlie Birchill and Mel Gaynor of Simple Minds to record the song. Jim Kerr suggested that he and Baz alternate the vocals and the eighth run-through was recorded. There were no overdubs – it was completely live. It was available as a one-sided seven-inch single on white vinyl from the Simple Minds website on 6 November 2015.

Compilations

The Stranglers' back catalogue has been plundered mercilessly over the years. Rest assured that I'm not going to trawl through all of these, but I will talk about some of the important ones and one unreleased compilation. Many of the compilations issued contain more or less the same tracks and some have even charted.

IV (1980)
Label: IRS Records
Ironically, the first Stranglers compilation album was only released in the United States and Canada on 24 September 1980. It contained five tracks from *The Raven,* which had not been released in the US and five other tracks. There was a free single also with four tracks: 'Choosey Susie' and 'Straighten Out' by the band, plus 'White Room' from Hugh's album *Nosferatu* and a live track from JJ, 'Ode To Joy'/'Do The European', which had been previously unreleased.

The Collection 1977–1982 (1982)
Label: Liberty Records
This was released to complete the band's contract with EMI. The 14 tracks contained The Stranglers' most popular singles and album tracks thus far and a new song, 'Strange Little Girl', which the band had submitted to EMI in 1974. The re-recorded version became a top ten hit. This compilation reached number 12 in the UK album charts and was awarded a silver disc for sales. This album is in the running for the worst album sleeve ever award, with the black-clad girl – you know the one.

Off The Beaten Track (1986)
Label: Liberty Records
A 13-track collection of B-Sides and singles that didn't appear on the albums between 1977 and 1982. It reached number 80 on the album charts.

Singles (The UA Years) (1989)
Label: Liberty Records
Another 'Best of' from the back catalogue of 1977 – 1982. This 20-track collection reached number 57 on the Album Charts.

Greatest Hits 1977-1990 (1990)
Label: Epic Records
Only 15 tracks in this collection, but it covers the singles from both EMI and Epic. Released in November 1990, this turned out to be the band's best-selling compilation, reaching number four in the charts. It sold over 300,000 copies, thereby earning the band a platinum disc. It was also the band's longest stay in the charts at 47 weeks.

The Old Testament: The U.A. Studio Recordings (1977–1982) (1992)

Label: EMI Records

This was a massive four-CD box set containing the band's first six studio albums and some non-album singles. It was reissued in 2013 as a five-disc set with the same contents, plus a bonus disc of rarities.

All Twelve Inches (1992)

Label: Epic Records

During the 1980s, 12" versions of singles were the rage and Epic decided to do the same with The Stranglers. There are a dozen tracks on this collection, all remixed for a 12" release. The period covered is 1983 to 1990.

The Early Years – 74-75-76 Rare Live And Unreleased (1992)

Label: Newspeak Records

Very much back in time for this one, with three tracks from a 1976 demo session ('Grip', 'Bitching' and 'Go Buddy Go'), a live track from The Railway Tavern in 1975 ('Princess Of The Streets'), nine tracks recorded live at The Hammersmith Odeon when the band were supporting Patti Smith and three tracks recorded as a demo in Fulham in 1974 ('Wasted', 'Strange Little Girl' and 'My Young Dreams'). These three songs from 1974 are the only known recordings that feature Hans Warmling. 'Strange Little Girl' was re-recorded later and became a hit, 'My Young Dreams' was released by A Marriage of Convenience (see *The Rarities*) and 'Wasted' appears never to have been recorded again.

Strangled From Birth And Beyond (1994)

Label: SIS

Released by The Stranglers Information Service to members of the Fan Club. Ten tracks overall: six rare tracks from The Stranglers, the Marriage of Convenience single and three solo JJ Burnel tracks. All these tracks turned up on *The Rarities* in 2002.

The Sessions (1995)

Label: Essential Records through Castle Communications

This collection contains 11 tracks recorded by the BBC for broadcast on Radio 1 between 1977 and 1982. 'Hanging Around', 'I Feel Like A Wog', 'Goodbye Toulouse' and 'Something Better Change' were produced by Jeff Griffin and were broadcast on 7 March 1977. 'Dead Ringer', 'No More Heroes' and 'Burning Up Time' were produced by Tony Wilson and broadcast on 13 September 1977. 'The Men They Love To Hate', 'Nuclear Device'/'Genetix' and 'Down In The Sewer' were produced by Dale Griffin and broadcast on 11 February 1982. The last three tracks were released as a CD single (see 'Live Recordings').

The Hit Men (1997)
Label: EMI
Released as part of EMI's 100th Birthday celebrations in February 1997, this two-CD, 43-track compilation contained selected tracks from the first ten studio albums, including non-album singles and the re-recorded 'Grip '89'. It reached number 116 in the album charts.

The Collection (1997)
Label: EMI Gold
EMI's budget catalogue label EMI Gold also got in on the act by releasing this 18-track compilation, which was essentially a 'best of' from the years 1977-1982.

Hits And Heroes (1999)
Label: EMI
A two-CD, 37-track compilation of hits and rarities covering the period 1977-1982. Some Radio Edits and 12" versions are included.

The UA Singles '77-79' (2001)
Label: EMI
This ten-CD box set contains all the singles released by the band, from 'Grip' to 'Duchess', in facsimiles of the original sleeves. The singles that were issued free with the albums are also included.

Peaches: The Very Best Of The Stranglers (2002)
Label: EMI
EMI continued to issue compilations at an astounding rate and this one charted at number 22 and earned the Meninblack another gold disc. Another of the 'obvious' album covers with a tin of peaches, this houses 20 tracks, including 'Grip '89'. The running order seems a bit haphazard and is all over the place. Oh, and the tracklisting is upside down. It was also issued as a double vinyl album on 27 November 2020 on Parlophone Records.

The Rarities (2002)
Label: EMI
This does what it says on the tin. With 18 tracks overall, this includes all the tracks contained on *Strangled At Birth And Beyond*, plus the Celia and The Mutations tracks, foreign language versions, radio edits and demos.

The UA Singles '79-82' (2003)
Label: EMI
Like the earlier *77-79* collection, this is a ten-CD box set containing all the singles released by the band, from 'Nuclear Device' to 'Strange Little Girl', in facsimiles of the original sleeves. Two overseas releases are also included: the

Swedish release of 'Sverige', which had 'In The Shadows' on the B-side, and the French release of 'N'emmenes Pas Harry', with 'Livin' In A Bear Cage' on the flip.

The Story So Far (2007)
Label: EMI Gold
This compilation presents two CDs containing 36 tracks, but this time, we have four tracks recorded after the band's return to EMI. Two tracks, each from *Norfolk Coast* and *Suite XVI,* are included.

FortyTwoForty (2008) (unreleased)
Label: Sony/BMG
Tracklisting: 'All Day And All Of The Night', 'Always The Sun', 'Big Thing Coming', 'Duchess', 'European Female', 'Five Minutes', 'Go Buddy Go', 'Golden Brown', 'Let Me Down Easy', 'Midnight Summer Dream', 'Nice In Nice', 'Nice N' Sleazy', '96 Tears', 'No Mercy', 'No More Heroes', 'Peaches', 'Paradise', 'Shakin' Like A Leaf', 'Skin Deep', 'Strange Little Girl', 'Something Better Change', 'Spectre Of Love'
This is one album that was never released. It was due to be released to coincide with the 30th anniversary of the band's recording debut (which was 1977, but who's counting?), as it says on the cover 'Thirty Years Hard Labour'. The album's title refers to the band's 42 top 40 singles at this point. Promo CDs were sent out to journalists with the tracks in alphabetical order. The 2008 tour featured the cover image on t-shirts and the tour programme.

The UA Singles 1977-1982 (2009)
Label: EMI
A three-CD set with 49 tracks of complete singles and B-sides 1977-1982.

Decades Apart (2010)
Label: EMI
Although a number of reviewers, myself included, called this the 'definitive Stranglers collection', the only thing that sets it apart from all the others is that it brings the band's story up to date. It has three tracks from *Norfolk Coast*, two from *Suite XVI* and two brand-new tracks especially recorded for the collection: 'Retro Rockets' and 'I Don't See The World Like You Do'. It was released on 1 March 2010 and reached number 146 on the UK album chart.

Here And There: The Epic B-Sides Collection 1983-1991 (2014)
Label: Coursegood Ltd
Released by the band themselves, it coincided with their 40th anniversary. Some bright spark noticed that Epic had released all the A-sides on a compilation, as well as a CD of 12" versions. However, the B-sides had been generally ignored. As the 1980s progressed, the 12" versions of the singles

tended to contain more tracks, some of them live. This two-CD, 40-track behemoth put that oversight right. What's more, it contained all six chapters of the Vladimir saga, which included one episode that had never been released on record ('Vladimir & The Pearl').

Live Recordings

The Stranglers have released quite a number of live albums. To go through every offering would be nigh on impossible, so I have selected a few of the very best to look at in order of release.

Live (X Cert) (1979)

Personnel:
Jean-Jacques Burnel: bass guitar, vocals
Hugh Cornwell: guitar, vocals
Dave Greenfield: keyboards, vocals
Jet Black: drums
Producer: Martin Rushent
Original UK label and catalogue number: United Artists UAG 30224
Released: 23 February 1979
Highest chart position: UK: 7 (Silver)
Running time: 42.39

Released between *Black And White* and *The Raven*, this set captures the early Stranglers at their raw best before they headed into their experimental stage. It spent ten weeks in the UK charts, reaching number seven, and was awarded a silver disc.

The original vinyl release contained 11 tracks. 'Grip', 'Dagenham Dave', 'Burning Up Time', 'I Feel Like A Wog', 'Straighten Out' and '5 Minutes' were recorded at The Roundhouse in London on 5 November 1977. 'Dead Ringer' and 'Hanging Around' were recorded at the same venue on 6 November 1977 and 26 June 1977, respectively, and 'Curfew', 'Do You Wanna', 'Death And Night And Blood' and 'Go Buddy Go' were recorded at Battersea Park on 16 September 1978 (yes, the gig with the strippers).

When reissued on CD in 2001, seven more tracks were added. 'Pleasant In The Big Shitty' from The Nashville, London on 10 December 1976, which was originally released as a free 7" disc with the *Rattus Norvegicus* album; 'In The Shadows', recorded at The Hope and Anchor, London on 22 November 1977, which was included on the 'Don't Bring Harry' EP; 'Sometimes', 'Mean To Me', 'London Lady', 'Goodbye Toulouse' and a different version of 'Hanging Around' from around the same time as the Roundhouse shows.

The search for these tracks scuppered the whole 2001 reissue schedule. When Steve Woof and Alan G Parker were sorting out the reissue campaign, they wanted to put bonus tracks on every album. Unfortunately, there appeared to be no other live tracks that had survived. As this campaign was the first in what was hoped to be a long line, it was imperative that it was done correctly and Steve and Alan were of the opinion that if bonus tracks were not included on every reissue, EMI may pull the whole thing. Alan told me in 2023:

> I went home and had a 'eureka' moment. I found a Stranglers bootleg CD that I had bought at a record fair in Leeds and would you believe it, the

sound quality was clear as a bell, and they were all recorded in the same year as *X Certs*. I took them to Abbey Road Studios and engineer Ron Hill cleaned them up. It saved the day.

All Live And All Of The Night (1988)

Personnel:
Jean-Jacques Burnel: bass guitar, lead and backing vocals
Hugh Cornwell: guitar, lead and backing vocals
Dave Greenfield: keyboards, backing vocals
Jet Black: drums, percussion
Additional personnel:
Alex Gifford: saxophone, backing vocals
Jason Votier: trumpet, backing vocals
Chris Lawrence: trombone, backing vocals
Producer: The Stranglers and Ted Hayton
Original UK label and catalogue number: Epic EPC 460259
Released: 8 February 1988
Highest chart position: UK: 12 (Gold)
Running time: 50.59

Released between *Dreamtime* and *10*, the album spent six weeks in the UK charts, reaching number 12, and was awarded a gold disc. There were 13 tracks on the original vinyl release, which were recorded at Le Zenith, Paris (29 April 1985), Hammersmith Odeon, London (31 March 1987) and The Reading Festival (30 August 1987). However, the live version of The Kinks' 'All Day And All Of The Night' wasn't considered of suitable quality for the release and a 'live' version, specially recorded in the studio, was added instead.

In 1999, there was a CD reissue in Japan which included six bonus tracks and the proper live version of 'All Day And All Of The Night'. In 2001, the studio version was omitted and the live version was added (with another eight tracks) to an EMI reissue. These came from recordings made at The Palais Des Sports, Orleans (28 April 1985), St George's Hall, Bradford (2 March 1990), Guildford Civic Hall, Guildford (19 March 1990) and Alexandra Palace, London (11 August 1990).

'All Day And All Of The Night' was released as a single from the album on Epic Records (VICE 1) in December 1987 and reached number seven in the UK charts during a seven-week residency. The single also reached number three in Ireland and number 38 in New Zealand. The B-side was 'Viva Vlad!'. The tracks recorded in 1990 also feature John Ellis on second guitar.

The Radio 1 Sessions – The Evening Show (1989)

Personnel:
Jean-Jacques Burnel: bass guitar, vocals
Hugh Cornwell: guitar, vocals

Dave Greenfield: keyboards, vocals
Jet Black: drums
Producer: Dale Griffin
Original UK label and catalogue number: Strange Fruit SFNTCD020
Released: 1989
Highest chart position: n/a

A session recorded by the BBC on 24 January 1982 and transmitted on BBC Radio 1 on 11 February 1982. There were three tracks: 'The Man They Love To Hate' sung by JJ, an eight-minute track combining 'Nuclear Device' and 'Genetix' sung by Dave and Hugh and 'Down In The Sewer' sung by Hugh. It was released in 1989 as a CD single and on 12" vinyl. It didn't chart.

Live At The Hope And Anchor (1992)

Personnel:
Jean-Jacques Burnel: bass guitar, vocals
Hugh Cornwell: guitar, vocals
Dave Greenfield: keyboards, vocals
Jet Black: drums
Producer: Jean-Jacques Burnel
Original UK label and catalogue number: EMI 798789
Released: 9 March 1992
Highest chart position: n/a
Running time: 77.43

Originally only available as a bootleg, it received its first official release in 1992. This is the full Stranglers set (19 tracks) as recorded on the opening night of the 'Front Row Festival' at The Hope and Anchor pub in Islington, London on 22 November 1977.

Saturday Night, Sunday Morning

Personnel:
Jean-Jacques Burnel: bass guitar, vocals
Hugh Cornwell: guitar, vocals
Dave Greenfield: keyboards, vocals
Jet Black: drums
Additional personnel:
John Ellis: guitar
Original UK label and catalogue number: Castle Communications ESSLP 194
Released: June 1993
Highest chart position: UK: 29
Running time: 52.55

This was recorded at The Alexandra Palace on 11 August 1990 and was Hugh Cornwell's last show with the band, although nobody knew (except perhaps Hugh) at the time of recording. The album was mixed by Stuart MacMillan at Central Television Music Studio in Birmingham, with JJ, Dave and Jet in

attendance. A CD single was released by Epic (6564307) in January 1991, containing four tracks from the show: 'Always The Sun', 'Nuclear Device', 'All Day And All Of The Night' and 'Punch & Judy'. It spent five weeks in the charts, reaching number 29. A VHS Video was released, which contained a different tracklisting, and it was released on DVD in 1990 entitled *Live At Alexandra Palace*.

The Stranglers And Friends – Live In Concert (1995)

Personnel:
Jean-Jacques Burnel: bass guitar, vocals
Dave Greenfield: keyboards
Jet Black: drums
John Ellis: guitar
Additional personnel:
Steve Nisbett: rhythmic drum patterns
Robert Smith: guitar ('Grip' and 'Hanging Around')
Robert Fripp: guitar ('Tank', 'Threatened', 'Toiler On The Sea')
Basil Gabbidon: guitar ('The Raven', 'Nice And Sleazy')
Wilko Johnson: guitar ('Dead Loss Angeles', 'Bring On The Nubiles')
John Turnbull: guitar ('Peaches', 'Bear Cage')
Larry Wallis: guitar ('Five Minutes')
Steve Hillage: guitar ('Something Better Change', 'Down In The Sewer')
Matthieu Hartley: keyboards ('Bear Cage')
Nik Turner: saxophone ('Nice And Sleazy')
Davey Payne: saxophone ('Peaches', 'Bear Cage')
Hazel O'Connor: vocals ('Grip' and 'Hanging Around')
Peter Hammill: vocals ('Tank', 'The Raven')
Phil Daniels: vocals ('Toiler On The Sea', 'Dead Loss Angeles')
Nicky Tesco: vocals ('Nice And Sleazy')
Richard Jobson: vocals ('Bring On The Nubiles', 'No More Heroes', 'Five Minutes')
Toyah Willcox: vocals ('Duchess', 'Something Better Change'), backing vocals ('Peaches', 'Bear Cage')
Ian Dury: vocals ('Peaches', 'Bear Cage')
Jake Burns: vocals ('Down In The Sewer')
Producer: Martin Rushent
Original UK label and catalogue number: Receiver RRCD 195 (1995), Hallmark 302902 (1997), Castle Music 06076-81156-2 (2002)
Released: 21 February 1995
Highest chart position: n/a
Running time: 70.00
Tracklisting: 'Introduction', 'Grip', 'Hanging Around', 'Tank', 'Threatened', 'Toiler On The Sea', 'The Raven', 'Dead Loss Angeles', 'Nice And Sleazy', 'Bring On The Nubiles', 'Peaches', 'Bear Cage', 'Duchess', 'No More Heroes', 'Five Minutes', 'Something Better Change', 'Down In The Sewer'

During the spring of 1980, Hugh was spending time as a guest in the Pentonville Hotel for the possession of drugs. He wasn't released until 25 April. However, two gigs were scheduled at the Rainbow Theatre in London on 3 and 4 April. As Hugh was unable to perform, John Ellis was brought in to play guitar and the management approached a number of artists to fill in for Hugh. Also, Steve Nisbett, the drummer with reggae band Steel Pulse – who had supported The Stranglers on numerous occasions – supplied rhythmic drum patterns throughout. The second show, on the 4 April, was released as this album, although the Hallmark version contains four fewer tracks. The intention was to release an album of the event at the time, with the proceeds going to Cure, a drug rehabilitation scheme. Unfortunately, the band almost went bankrupt and the album was shelved.

Following an introduction by Jet Black, the band kicked off a memorable show. It is interesting to note that both Toyah Willcox and Robert Fripp performed at the shows, and considering they married in 1986, this author thought that it was at this concert that they met. However, Toyah told me in July 2023:

> When I performed with The Stranglers, it was a wonderful experience of chaos that somehow organised itself into a spectacular event. There were at least 80 people backstage each night, all trying to find a quiet corner, most of them artists on the front line of influence and success ... wildly exciting. I cannot say I met my husband Robert Fripp there; I certainly wasn't introduced to him and didn't perform any songs with him ... but there might be a finale picture out there where we are accidentally on stage together at the very end of the show with all the other artists. We would have been blissfully unaware of each other ... In a way, I wish I had met him at The Rainbow ... but he says he wasn't ready to deal with someone like me at that point in history!

Friday The Thirteenth (1999)
Personnel:
Jean-Jacques Burnel: bass guitar, vocals
Dave Greenfield: keyboards, vocals
Jet Black: drums
Paul Roberts: lead vocals
John Ellis: guitar, vocals
Additional personnel:
The Electra Strings
Jocelyn Pook: string co-ordination
Original UK label and catalogue number: Eagle Records EAGCD006
Released: 1999
Highest chart position: n/a
Running time: 66.04

This live album (originally suggested by JJ) was released to celebrate the 21st anniversary of the band's signing of their original recording contract with United Artists. And yes, it was recorded on Friday the 13th (13 June 1997) at The Royal Albert Hall in London. The band used the Manor Mobile Recording Studio to capture the event, which was also filmed and released on DVD with extra tracks. 'It was the first time I ever wore a suit on stage', quipped JJ at the time, whilst singer Paul Roberts became the first person to do a stage dive at the Royal Albert Hall, which resulted in him losing a show! Glamour was provided by the 18-piece Electra Strings – an all-female orchestra.

5 Live 01 (2001)
Personnel:
Jean-Jacques Burnel: bass guitar, vocals
Dave Greenfield: keyboards, vocals
Jet Black: drums
Paul Roberts: lead vocals
Baz Warne: guitar, vocals
Producer: Max Bisgrove
Original UK label and catalogue number: SPV Recordings SPV 085-71052-P DCD
Released: 29 January 2001
Highest chart position: n/a
Running time: 87.50
Recorded live at ARC Music Studio in Hamburg, this double CD containing 25 tracks covers the whole of the band's career thus far. It's also the first release to feature the new guitarist Baz Warne, who had recently replaced the departing John Ellis.

Coast To Coast (2005)
Personnel:
Jean-Jacques Burnel: bass guitar, vocals
Dave Greenfield: keyboards
Jet Black: drums, percussion
Paul Roberts: lead vocals
Baz Warne: guitar, vocals
Producer: Louie Nicastro
Original UK label and catalogue number: Coursegood CG003
Released: 20 February 2005
Highest chart position: n/a
Running time: 67.35
Released on the band's own label, these tracks – as the title suggests – were recorded on the UK tour to promote the album *Norfolk Coast* in March 2004. Of the 18 tracks, eight of the new album's 11 tracks were performed. This was the last release to feature Paul Roberts.

Themeninblackinbrugge (2008)
Personnel:
Jean-Jacques Burnel: acoustic bass, acoustic guitar, vocals
Dave Greenfield: keyboards, acoustic guitar, backing vocals
Jet Black: drums
Baz Warne: acoustic guitar, vocals, harmonica
Additional personnel:
Neil Sparkes: percussion, backing vocals
John MacMillan: accordion (on 'Waltzinblack')
Producer: Louie Nicastro
Original UK label and catalogue number: Coursegood CG004
Released: 2008
Highest chart position: n/a
As the band members got a little older, they decided to try something new. A lot of bands were incorporating acoustic sections during live gigs, so our heroes decided to play a full concert acoustically. As Jet had gone into semi-retirement in 2007, he had support from Neil Sparkes, who helped out in the live shows from 2007 to 2012. Some excellent arrangements and vocal harmonies are showcased here, as The Stranglers' music translates effectively into a more relaxed experience. The show was recorded on 23 November 2007 at the Stadsschouwberg Cultuurecentrum, Bruges, Belgium.

Giants (2012)
Personnel:
Jean-Jacques Burnel: bass guitar, vocals
Dave Greenfield: keyboards, vocals
Jet Black: drums
Baz Warne: guitar, vocals
Producer: Louie Nicastro
Original UK label and catalogue number: Absolute CDCG005
Released: 5 March 2012
Highest chart position: n/a
This was included as a bonus disc with the 'deluxe' version of *Giants*. There are 14 acoustic tracks recorded at the 'Weekendinblack' Stranglers Convention on 19 and 20 November 2011 at the Camden Centre in London.

Feel It Live (2013)
Personnel:
Jean-Jacques Burnel: bass guitar, vocals
Dave Greenfield: keyboards, vocals
Jet Black: drums
Baz Warne: guitar, vocals
Producer: Louie Nicastro
Original UK label and catalogue number: Coursegood CG007

Released: 30 June 2013
Highest chart position: n/a
A live CD of 21 tracks recorded at various venues during the *Giants* tour of 2012 featuring six tracks from the album.

Black And White Live (2016)
Personnel:
Jean-Jacques Burnel: bass guitar, vocals
Dave Greenfield: keyboards, vocals
Jet Black: drums, vocals (on 'Old Codger')
Baz Warne: guitar, vocals
Additional personnel:
Jim Macaulay: drums (on 'Tank', 'Toiler On The Sea', 'Threatened' and 'Enough Time')
Neil Sparkes: drums (on 'Walk On By' and 'Tits')
John Ellis: guitar (on 'Old Codger')
Tim Bruce: drums (on 'Old Codger')
Producer: Louie Nicastro
Original UK label and catalogue number: Coursegood CG010
Released: March 2016
Highest chart position: n/a
During March 2016, The Stranglers performed their third album *Black And White* live and in full for the very first time. To accompany the tour, a CD made up of songs performed at different shows was compiled for sale at the concerts, with all the tracks from the original album, plus some tracks from the same time (B-sides, etc.) and a studio recording of one of the tracks. Some of the recordings had been available previously on other live CDs, but seven of the 17 tracks were previously unreleased.

Rattus Relived (2017)
Personnel:
Jean-Jacques Burnel: bass guitar, vocals
Dave Greenfield: keyboards, vocals
Jet Black: drums, percussion
Baz Warne: guitar, vocals
Additional personnel:
Neil Sparkes: percussion (on 'English Towns')
Original UK label and catalogue number: Coursegood CG011
Released: 2017
Highest chart position: n/a
Another CD that was released for sale at gigs. The 20 tracks include live versions of tracks from the first two albums (and associated singles) – nine from *Rattus Norvegicus* and 11 from *No More Heroes*. All the tracks were recorded at The Roundhouse, London, on 4 November 2007, except 'Down In

The Sewer, which was recorded on 19 March 2010 at the Hammersmith Odeon, and 'English Towns', which was taken from the album *Themeninblackinbrugge*.

Themeninblackintokyo (2021)
Personnel:
Jean-Jacques Burnel: bass guitar, vocals
Dave Greenfield: keyboards, vocals
Baz Warne: guitar, vocals
Jim Macaulay: drums, vocals
Original UK label and catalogue number: Coursegood CGCD13
Released: 3 December 2021
Highest chart position: n/a
A double CD of 22 live tracks covering the whole history of the band to date and recorded at Tsutaya O-West in Tokyo on 5 November 2019. This would turn out to be the last concert performed by The Stranglers in Japan with keyboard player Dave Greenfield.

Dave Greenfield – A Tribute (2021)
Personnel:
Jean-Jacques Burnel: bass guitar, vocals
Dave Greenfield: keyboards, backing vocals, lead vocals on 'Dead Ringer', 'Peasant In The Big Shitty', 'Do You Wanna?' and 'Four Horsemen'
Baz Warne: guitar, vocals
Jim Macaulay: drums, backing vocals
Producer: Louie Nicastro
Original UK label and catalogue number: Coursegood DPGCD1
Released: 10 September 2021
Highest chart position: n/a
People who pre-ordered the album *Dark Matters* through The Stranglers' official store also received this eight-track CD, which celebrates the talent of keyboard player Dave Greenfield, who sadly passed away on 3 May 2020. He was in hospital being treated for a heart-related problem when he contracted COVID-19. Of the eight songs, all taken from different live shows, Dave features as lead vocalist on four.

Fifty Years In Black – The Anniversary Tour 2024 (2024)
Personnel:
Jean-Jacques Burnel: bass guitar, vocals
Baz Warne: guitar, vocals
Jim Macaulay: drums, percussion
Toby Hounsham: keyboards, vocals
Released: 16 August 2024 (TBC)
In April 2024, it was announced that The Stranglers intended to release a triple live album on gold-coloured vinyl, later in 2024. It was described as a

chronological audio diary' of the 50th-anniversary tour of the UK and Ireland, and it features the whole set list from the tour with two tracks from every date except Bristol, as that date was rearranged, and London that has six tracks from the Royal Albert Hall gig.

The album will be mixed and mastered by Louie Nicastro, who was the sound engineer for the tour and also the band's producer. The band's manager, Sil Willcox, told the author that the decision as to whether to release the set on CD hadn't at that stage been made.

Solo Recordings

This is a selected list of the studio albums released by members of The Stranglers either during or after their tenure in the band.

J.J. Burnel

Euroman Cometh (1979), *Un Jour Parfait* (1988), *Gankutsuou: The Count Of Monte Cristo* (2005) – with Kasamatsu Kouji

Dave Greenfield and J.J. Burnel

Fire & Water (Ecoutez Vos Murs) (1983)

Baz Warne

Sun Devils (2001) – with Sun Devils, *Common Thread* (2002), *Wingmen* (2023) – with Wingmen (Baz, Paul Gray, Leigh Heggarty and Marty Love)

Hugh Cornwell

Nosferatu (1979) – with Robert Williams, *Wolf* (1988), *CCW* (1992, UFO) – as CCW (Hugh with Roger Cook and Andy West), *Wired* (1993), *Guilty* (1997), *Hi Fi* (2001), *Footprints In The Desert* (2002), *Beyond Elysian Fields* (2004), *Hooverdam* (2008), *Totem And Taboo* (2012), *Monster* – 2CD (2018) (includes bonus disc of acoustic versions of Stranglers songs), *Moments Of Madness* (2022)

The Purple Helmets (J.J. Burnel, Dave Greenfield And John Ellis)

Ride Again (1988), *Rise Again* (1989)

Paul Roberts

Self Discovery (2001) (as the Faith Band), *The Pressure Sensitive* (2003) (as the Faith Band), *End Games* (2007) (as Soulsec)

John Ellis

Destination Everywhere (Gallery Music #3) (1995), *Our Internal Monologue (Gallery Music #4)* (1995), *Shock Of Contact (Gallery Music #5)* (1996), *Acrylic* (1997), *Spic 'N' Span* (1999), *Wabi Sabi 21©* (2009), *Sly Guitar* (2013), *Past, Present And Into The Future* (2017) – with The Vibrators, *Mars Casino* (2019) – with The Vibrators & Chris Spedding

The Stranglers On DVD

As with the compilations and solo work, this isn't a complete list, but these are, in my opinion, the best and most representative of those released.

Saturday Night, Sunday Morning (1999)
Originally released in 1990 on VHS, this was reissued in 1999 as a DVD entitled 'Live at Alexandra Palace'. This is a film of Hugh's final gig with the band.

The Video Collection 1977–1982 (2001)
Originally released on VHS in 1982, it was issued on DVD in 2001. It features almost an hour of 16 Stranglers hits, from 'Grip' to 'Strange Little Girl'.

Friday The Thirteenth (1997)
The film of the 1997 concert at The Royal Albert Hall. It contains half a dozen more tracks than the CD, including a rare live outing of 'Summer In The City'.

Live '78, SF (2005)
Half an hour of early Stranglers in the form of seven tracks recorded in San Francisco.

Rattus At The Roundhouse (2007)
In November 2007, The Stranglers returned to The Roundhouse in London, 30 years after their last visit, with a set based on the original 1977 *Heroes* tour.

Live At The Apollo (2010)
Filmed during the *Decades Apart* tour at the Hammersmith Odeon, this DVD was fan-funded and contained a booklet of the names of the fans who contributed. Containing 17 tracks and six bonus tracks, this also includes a 17-track CD of the show.

Never To Look Back: The Video Collection 1983-2012 (2013)
Seventeen hits from 'European Female' to 'Mercury Rising', plus a plethora of live tracks. An information booklet was available free from the band's website.

The Ruby Tour 2014 (2014)
Recorded at the Paris Olympia on 7 April 2014, these 27 tracks featured on *The Ruby* tour. As Jet Black didn't tour abroad at that time, the last four tracks were recorded at The Manchester Academy on 29 March 2014, this time with Jet on the drums.

Postscript

After Dave Greenfield's passing, JJ Burnel was now the sole remaining original member of The Stranglers. With Pam Greenfield's blessing, they decided to honour the tour that had been planned pre-Covid. The main problem was that they had no keyboard player. The band needed someone who could be truthful to the work of Dave, and they found the person in the form of Toby Hounsham. Toby was born in Clevedon, Somerset, on 19 July 1972. Originally in the 1990s band Rialto, Toby had been a professional musician for over 30 years and played regularly with Ray Dorset of Mungo Jerry fame, as well as Go West and Katrina (of Katrina and the Waves). He played his first live dates with the band in France and was immediately accepted by the fans. JJ told me in 2022: 'He treats everything Dave played with great respect, and he keeps saying, "I can't believe I'm playing with the best band in the world"'. The tour was a great success, but it had been, according to the band, the last full tour by The Stranglers. They did not want to do big tours anymore but would do the odd date and festival. However, *The Fifty Years Of Black* tour of the UK took place in March 2024, with dates in France, Belgium, Germany and The Netherlands in October. The band played two sets, the first half being the 'longer' songs and the second being more of the hits and fan favourites. As they wanted to play more songs from their career, the band opted not to have a support act (apart from the gig at The Royal Albert Hall in London). The total set ran to 29 songs. And for the future? Well, according to both JJ and Baz, they have hundreds of songs part written. So, we have probably not heard the last from The Stranglers.

Bibliography And Selected Reading

Black, J., *Much Ado About Nothing* (Stranglers Information Service, 1981)
Black, J., *Seven Days In Nice* (Coursegood Books, 2011)
Boile, A., *Jean-Jacques Burnel – Strangler In The Light* (Coursegood Books, 2023)
Buckley, D., *No Mercy* (Hodder & Stoughton, 1997)
Clarke, D. (editor), *The Penguin Encyclopedia Of Popular Music* (Penguin, 1998)
Cornwell, H., Drury, J., *The Stranglers – Song By Song* (Sanctuary Publishing, 2001)
Finnigan, M., Rodgers, D., *The Stranglers 1977-90 – A Musical Critique* (Wymer Publishing, 2023)
Houghton, R., *The Stranglers Live (Excerpts) – The Story Of The Stranglers As Told By The Fans* (This Day In Music, 2022)
Larkin, C., *Virgin Encyclopedia Of 60s Music* (Virgin, 2002)
Perry, A., Emberton, S., *The Stranglers – Then And Now* (Wymer Publishing, 2018)
Rees, D., Crampton, L., *Q Book Of Punk Legends* (given away with issue 116 of *Q Magazine*, 1996)
Rees, D., Crampton, L., (editors), *Q Encyclopedia Of Rock Stars* (Dorling Kindersley, 1999)
Roberts, D. (editor), *Guinness Book Of British Hit Singles & Albums* (Guinness World Records, 2003)
Shenton, L., *The Stranglers – 1977* (Wymer Publishing, 2021)
Shenton, L., *The Stranglers – La Folie* (Wymer Publishing, 2022)
Tobler, J., *New Musical Express Rock 'N' Roll Years* (Hamlyn, 1992)
Visconti, T., *Bowie, Bolan And The Brooklyn Boy* (Harper Collins, 2007)
White, G.R., *British Hit EPs 1955-1989* (Music Mentor Books, 2014)

CD Liner notes by Alan Parker, Chris Twomey, Nik Yeomans, Neil Martin, Marian Shepherd and Ralph Tritt.

Also available from Sonicbond

On Track Series

Allman Brothers Band – Andrew Wild 978-1-78952-252-5
Tori Amos – Lisa Torem 978-1-78952-142-9
Aphex Twin – Beau Waddell 978-1-78952-267-9
Asia – Peter Braidis 978-1-78952-099-6
Badfinger – Robert Day-Webb 978-1-878952-176-4
Barclay James Harvest – Keith And Monica Domone 978-1-78952-067-5
Beck – Arthur Lizie 978-1-78952-258-7
The Beatles – Andrew Wild 978-1-78952-009-5
The Beatles Solo 1969-1980 – Andrew Wild 978-1-78952-030-9
Blue Oyster Cult – Jacob Holm-Lupo 978-1-78952-007-1
Blur – Matt Bishop 978-178952-164-1
Marc Bolan And T.rex – Peter Gallagher 978-1-78952-124-5
Kate Bush – Bill Thomas 978-1-78952-097-2
Camel – Hamish Kuzminski 978-1-78952-040-8
Captain Beefheart – Opher Goodwin 978-1-78952-235-8
Caravan – Andy Boot 978-1-78952-127-6
Cardiacs – Eric Benac 978-1-78952-131-3
Nick Cave And The Bad Seeds – Dominic Sanderson 978-1-78952-240-2
Eric Clapton Solo – Andrew Wild 978-1-78952-141-2
The Clash – Nick Assirati 978-1-78952-077-4
Elvis Costello And The Attractions – Georg Purvis 978-1-78952-129-0
Crosby, Stills & Nash – Andrew Wild 978-1-78952-039-2
Creedence Clearwater Revival – Tony Thompson 978-178952-237-2
The Damned – Morgan Brown 978-1-78952-136-8
Deep Purple And Rainbow 1968-79 – Steve Pilkington 978-1-78952-002-6
Dire Straits – Andrew Wild 978-1-78952-044-6
The Doors – Tony Thompson 978-1-78952-137-5
Dream Theater – Jordan Blum 978-1-78952-050-7
Eagles – John Van Der Kiste 978-1-78952-260-0
Earth, Wind And Fire – Bud Wilkins 978-1-78952-272-3
Electric Light Orchestra – Barry Delve 978-1-78952-152-8
Emerson Lake And Palmer – Mike Goode 978-1-78952-000-2
Fairport Convention – Kevan Furbank 978-1-78952-051-4
Peter Gabriel – Graeme Scarfe 978-1-78952-138-2
Genesis – Stuart Macfarlane 978-1-78952-005-7
Gentle Giant – Gary Steel 978-1-78952-058-3
Gong – Kevan Furbank 978-1-78952-082-8
Green Day – William E. Spevack 978-1-78952-261-7
Hall And Oates – Ian Abrahams 978-1-78952-167-2
Hawkwind – Duncan Harris 978-1-78952-052-1
Peter Hammill – Richard Rees Jones 978-1-78952-163-4
Roy Harper – Opher Goodwin 978-1-78952-130-6

Jimi Hendrix – Emma Stott 978-1-78952-175-7
The Hollies – Andrew Darlington 978-1-78952-159-7
Horslips – Richard James 978-1-78952-263-1
The Human League And The Sheffield Scene –
Andrew Darlington 978-1-78952-186-3
The Incredible String Band – Tim Moon 978-1-78952-107-8
Iron Maiden – Steve Pilkington 978-1-78952-061-3
Joe Jackson – Richard James 978-1-78952-189-4
Jefferson Airplane – Richard Butterworth 978-1-78952-143-6
Jethro Tull – Jordan Blum 978-1-78952-016-3
Elton John In The 1970s – Peter Kearns 978-1-78952-034-7
Billy Joel – Lisa Torem 978-1-78952-183-2
Judas Priest – John Tucker 978-1-78952-018-7
Kansas – Kevin Cummings 978-1-78952-057-6
The Kinks – Martin Hutchinson 978-1-78952-172-6
Korn – Matt Karpe 978-1-78952-153-5
Led Zeppelin – Steve Pilkington 978-1-78952-151-1
Level 42 – Matt Philips 978-1-78952-102-3
Little Feat – Georg Purvis - 978-1-78952-168-9
Aimee Mann – Jez Rowden 978-1-78952-036-1
Joni Mitchell – Peter Kearns 978-1-78952-081-1
The Moody Blues – Geoffrey Feakes 978-1-78952-042-2
Motorhead – Duncan Harris 978-1-78952-173-3
Nektar – Scott Meze – 978-1-78952-257-0
New Order – Dennis Remmer – 978-1-78952-249-5
Nightwish – Simon Mcmurdo – 978-1-78952-270-9
Laura Nyro – Philip Ward 978-1-78952-182-5
Mike Oldfield – Ryan Yard 978-1-78952-060-6
Opeth – Jordan Blum 978-1-78-952-166-5
Pearl Jam – Ben L. Connor 978-1-78952-188-7
Tom Petty – Richard James 978-1-78952-128-3
Pink Floyd – Richard Butterworth 978-1-78952-242-6
The Police – Pete Braidis 978-1-78952-158-0
Porcupine Tree – Nick Holmes 978-1-78952-144-3
Queen – Andrew Wild 978-1-78952-003-3
Radiohead – William Allen 978-1-78952-149-8
Rancid – Paul Matts 989-1-78952-187-0
Renaissance – David Detmer 978-1-78952-062-0
Reo Speedwagon – Jim Romag 978-1-78952-262-4
The Rolling Stones 1963-80 – Steve Pilkington 978-1-78952-017-0
The Smiths And Morrissey – Tommy Gunnarsson 978-1-78952-140-5
Spirit – Rev. Keith A. Gordon – 978-1-78952- 248-8
Stackridge – Alan Draper 978-1-78952-232-7

Status Quo The Frantic Four Years – Richard James 978-1-78952-160-3
Steely Dan – Jez Rowden 978-1-78952-043-9
Steve Hackett – Geoffrey Feakes 978-1-78952-098-9
Tears For Fears – Paul Clark - 978-178952-238-9
Thin Lizzy – Graeme Stroud 978-1-78952-064-4
Tool – Matt Karpe 978-1-78952-234-1
Toto – Jacob Holm-Lupo 978-1-78952-019-4
U2 – Eoghan Lyng 978-1-78952-078-1
Ufo – Richard James 978-1-78952-073-6
Van Der Graaf Generator – Dan Coffey 978-1-78952-031-6
Van Halen – Morgan Brown – 9781-78952-256-3
The Who – Geoffrey Feakes 978-1-78952-076-7
Roy Wood And The Move – James R Turner 978-1-78952-008-8
Yes – Stephen Lambe 978-1-78952-001-9
Frank Zappa 1966 To 1979 – Eric Benac 978-1-78952-033-0
Warren Zevon – Peter Gallagher 978-1-78952-170-2
10cc – Peter Kearns 978-1-78952-054-5

Decades Series
The Bee Gees In The 1960s – Andrew Mon Hughes Et Al 978-1-78952-148-1
The Bee Gees In The 1970s – Andrew Mon Hughes Et Al 978-1-78952-179-5
Black Sabbath In The 1970s – Chris Sutton 978-1-78952-171-9
Britpop – Peter Richard Adams And Matt Pooler 978-1-78952-169-6
Phil Collins In The 1980s – Andrew Wild 978-1-78952-185-6
Alice Cooper In The 1970s – Chris Sutton 978-1-78952-104-7
Alice Cooper In The 1980s – Chris Sutton 978-1-78952-259-4
Curved Air In The 1970s – Laura Shenton 978-1-78952-069-9
Donovan In The 1960s – Jeff Fitzgerald 978-1-78952-233-4
Bob Dylan In The 1980s – Don Klees 978-1-78952-157-3
Brian Eno In The 1970s – Gary Parsons 978-1-78952-239-6
Faith No More In The 1990s – Matt Karpe 978-1-78952-250-1
Fleetwood Mac In The 1970s – Andrew Wild 978-1-78952-105-4
Fleetwood Mac In The 1980s – Don Klees 978-178952-254-9
Focus In The 1970s – Stephen Lambe 978-1-78952-079-8
Free And Bad Company In The 1970s – John Van Der Kiste 978-1-78952-178-8
Genesis In The 1970s – Bill Thomas 978178952-146-7
George Harrison In The 1970s – Eoghan Lyng 978-1-78952-174-0
Kiss In The 1970s – Peter Gallagher 978-1-78952-246-4
Manfred Mann's Earth Band In The 1970s – John Van Der Kiste 978178952-243-3
Marillion In The 1980s – Nathaniel Webb 978-1-78952-065-1
Van Morrison In The 1970s – Peter Childs - 978-1-78952-241-9
Mott The Hoople And Ian Hunter In The 1970s –

John Van Der Kiste 978-1-78-952-162-7
Pink Floyd In The 1970s – Georg Purvis 978-1-78952-072-9
Suzi Quatro In The 1970s – Darren Johnson 978-1-78952-236-5
Queen In The 1970s – James Griffiths 978-1-78952-265-5
Roxy Music In The 1970s – Dave Thompson 978-1-78952-180-1
Slade In The 1970s – Darren Johnson 978-1-78952-268-6
Status Quo In The 1980s – Greg Harper 978-1-78952-244-0
Tangerine Dream In The 1970s – Stephen Palmer 978-1-78952-161-0
The Sweet In The 1970s – Darren Johnson 978-1-78952-139-9
Uriah Heep In The 1970s – Steve Pilkington 978-1-78952-103-0
Van Der Graaf Generator In The 1970s – Steve Pilkington 978-1-78952-245-7
Rick Wakeman In The 1970s – Geoffrey Feakes 978-1-78952-264-8
Yes In The 1980s – Stephen Lambe With David Watkinson 978-1-78952-125-2

On Screen Series

Carry On... – Stephen Lambe 978-1-78952-004-0
David Cronenberg – Patrick Chapman 978-1-78952-071-2
Doctor Who: The David Tennant Years – Jamie Hailstone 978-1-78952-066-8
James Bond – Andrew Wild 978-1-78952-010-1
Monty Python – Steve Pilkington 978-1-78952-047-7
Seinfeld Seasons 1 To 5 – Stephen Lambe 978-1-78952-012-5

Other Books

1967: A Year In Psychedelic Rock 978-1-78952-155-9
1970: A Year In Rock – John Van Der Kiste 978-1-78952-147-4
1973: The Golden Year Of Progressive Rock 978-1-78952-165-8
Babysitting A Band On The Rocks – G.d. Praetorius 978-1-78952-106-1
Eric Clapton Sessions – Andrew Wild 978-1-78952-177-1
Derek Taylor: For Your Radioactive Children –
Andrew Darlington 978-1-78952-038-5
The Golden Road: The Recording History Of The Grateful Dead – John Kilbride 978-1-78952-156-6
Iggy And The Stooges On Stage 1967-1974 – Per Nilsen 978-1-78952-101-6
Jon Anderson And The Warriors – The Road To Yes –
David Watkinson 978-1-78952-059-0
Magic: The David Paton Story – David Paton 978-1-78952-266-2
Misty: The Music Of Johnny Mathis – Jakob Baekgaard 978-1-78952-247-1
Nu Metal: A Definitive Guide – Matt Karpe 978-1-78952-063-7
Tommy Bolin: In And Out Of Deep Purple – Laura Shenton 978-1-78952-070-5
Maximum Darkness – Deke Leonard 978-1-78952-048-4
The Twang Dynasty – Deke Leonard 978-1-78952-049-1

And Many More To Come!

Would you like to write for Sonicbond Publishing?

At Sonicbond Publishing we are always on the look-out for authors, particularly for our two main series:

On Track. Mixing fact with in depth analysis, the On Track series examines the work of a particular musical artist or group. All genres are considered from easy listening and jazz to 60s soul to 90s pop, via rock and metal.

On Screen. This series looks at the world of film and television. Subjects considered include directors, actors and writers, as well as entire television and film series. As with the On Track series, we balance fact with analysis.

While professional writing experience would, of course, be an advantage the most important qualification is to have real enthusiasm and knowledge of your subject. First-time authors are welcomed, but the ability to write well in English is essential.

Sonicbond Publishing has distribution throughout Europe and North America, and all books are also published in E-book form. Authors will be paid a royalty based on sales of their book.

Further details are available from www.sonicbondpublishing.co.uk. To contact us, complete the contact form there or email info@sonicbondpublishing.co.uk